Also by Leo Black

How To Analyze People at a Glance - Learn 15 Unmistakable Signals Others Put Off Without Realizing It and What They Mean

Suggestion: Secrets of Covert Manipulation

Secrets of Covert Manipulation

What You Need to Know to Exert More Influence and Affirm Your Needs Through Dark Psychology Techniques to Plant Subliminal Commands and Influence Others Without Detection

Leo Black

© Copyright 2020 - All rights reserved.

The content contained within this book may not be reproduced, duplicated or transmitted without direct written permission from the author or the publisher.

Under no circumstances will any blame or legal responsibility be held against the publisher, or author, for any damages, reparation, or monetary loss due to the information contained within this book, either directly or indirectly.

Legal Notice:

This book is copyright protected. It is only for personal use. You cannot amend, distribute, sell, use, quote or paraphrase any part, or the content within this book, without the consent of the author or publisher.

Disclaimer Notice:

Please note the information contained within this document is for educational and entertainment purposes only. All effort has been executed to present accurate, up to date, reliable, complete information. No warranties of any kind are declared or implied. Readers acknowledge that the author is not engaged in the rendering of legal, financial, medical or professional advice. The content within this book has been derived from various sources. Please consult a licensed professional before attempting any techniques outlined in this book.

By reading this document, the reader agrees that under no circumstances is the author responsible for any losses, direct or indirect, that are incurred as a result of the use of the information contained within this document, including, but not limited to, errors, omissions, or inaccuracies.

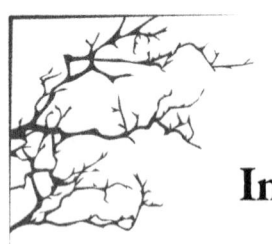

Introduction

"You are a manipulator. I like to think of myself more as an outcome engineer."

- J. R. Ward

Two girls begin to behave strangely in a small town in Massachusetts. For no apparent reason, they start having fits, vomiting, and claiming to see visions. They begin to scream uncontrollably, forcing everyone nearby to stare in horror. When a local doctor is called, he does not know what else to do but diagnose the fits as something he dreads to say: bewitchment.

Soon, many other girls have the same strange fits. People start to get worried as they appear out of nowhere, and no pure girl is safe. The town drew its people together to find the person responsible for these actions. The first two girls begin to scream and convulse when Tituba takes the stand. There is now no shadow of a doubt that she is the one causing the mayhem.

Perhaps in a desperate attempt to save her life as an informer, Tituba confesses to being a witch and claims there are others in the village that have her same powers, but she is the only one who can accurately recognize them.

Many others are accused and found guilty of witchcraft, flooding the courts and preventing long cases. Whoever confesses to being a witch is tried and put to death. Bridget Bishop

SUGGESTION: SECRETS OF COVERT MANIPULATION

is hung by the neck and Giles Corey is crushed between two stones until dead.

If this story seems familiar, you may have heard it before, perhaps in a classroom. Two girls were able to convince an entire town they were able to tell if someone was a witch. The Salem Witch Trials were some of the most horrifying and most remembered killings in United States history, and it was all thanks to the terror two girls inflicted on an easily-manipulated town.

You can use manipulation for good or for bad, but there is nothing inherently wrong with a little persuasion. In fact, persuasion can increase trust and understanding. However, many use the techniques contained here for selfish needs. The key to getting the right balance between good and bad is to search for your intent.

Have you ever felt the need to help a friend that was dying to become something they were not but did not have the courage to take the leap? What about seeing a friend's marriage crumble due to a lack of communication or trust in each other? Have you ever considered you might be able to get that promotion at work if you only had a solid strategy that could get you in the right circles? People have been using manipulation for millennia to change lives for good or bad. In its essence, though, manipulation is about changing beliefs.

The word "manipulation" has a negative connotation because people do not know how to use it. Many think of it as a way to influence people to do whatever they want, regardless of the consequences, but that could not be further from the truth. If done correctly, manipulation can be an effective way to persuade people to improve their lives or encourage people to pursue their dreams.

There are far too few good manipulators in the world for the sole reason that many people do not know effective techniques. However, manipulation is very easy once you get the hang of it. All it takes is a little practice. And the best place to start is here.

Psychology has been honing manipulative techniques for years. For example, you may not have even realized the color of this cover drove you to this title. You may not have realized that, when a friend suggested this book to you, you were subtly manipulated into taking a chance. The use of color, font, or persuasion from a friend is enough to have brought you here, and you can use these techniques and more to build a basis in human understanding.

Secrets of Covert Manipulation: What You Need to Know to Exert More Influence and Affirm Your Needs Through Dark Psychology Techniques to Plant Subliminal Commands and Influence Others Without Detection was written with all readers in mind. Whether you have a problem with a coworker or simply want to find out how much you can do without detection, you can adjust your behaviors to suit others and get further in life.

This book uses dark psychology techniques to aid in changing your future. Deception of the mind challenges and makes others believe they see what they cannot, and many people use these forms to perform magic tricks or imitate mind-reading. Through distraction, they are able to convince anyone.

The techniques listed in this book have been backed up by psychology and science, and each has proven to work. Studies conducted about manipulation have effectively changed the way we think about manipulation and improved the tactics needed to persuade.

This book is only a stepping stone into what you could achieve with dark psychology. Do not be afraid to experiment with the tactics used here. It is ultimately up to you how much you can learn from this book. Follow the suggestions to learn more about yourself and others. Practice the talents you learn before you start working on a long project. People change frequently, so it is up to you to adapt to changes in yours and others' lives. When you continue to practice, manipulation will become second nature to you, making your transition between techniques easy and effortless.

About the Author

Leo Black grew up as a shy boy. The subject of bullying, he had to struggle with a serious social phobia during his college years. He recognized how the inability to communicate properly with others was affecting opportunities and literally destroying his life.

Determined to turn his life around, Leo pushed himself out of his comfort zone. He forced casual conversations with others and used each one as a learning opportunity. Eventually, he identified patterns in body language, gestures and the tone of the voice that gave him essential information about every single person he was interacting with.

Fascinated by the extensiveness and complexity of human interactions, Leo obtained his Master of Psychological Science degree from Tulane University. He later on completed a doctorate program in cognitive/behavioral neuroscience.

What started as a simple personal passion was quickly transformed into a career path, a successful one at that! Leo

Black has worked with dozens of patients and clients through the years, helping them overcome confidence issues, clinical depression, body image disorders and various other conditions.

You can learn more about Leo Black's approach to analyzing people in his book, as well as in his personal blog.

Chapter 1: The Basics of Dark Psychology and Manipulation

For years, many have struggled to understand how truly great manipulators affect those around them. The way masters of dark psychology affect those around them can seem almost magical and, in many cases, they are. Words are profoundly influential to instruct and command, speak kindly or with derision. And learning the basics of dark psychology and manipulation can not only help you understand when you are being manipulated but also gives you the power to manipulate others.

What Is Manipulation?

The study of dark psychology delves deeply into the souls of darkly-minded people. Arsonists, necrophiles, serial killers, narcissism, and Machiavellianism, some of the most deeply disturbed members of society, conduct bizarre and often damaging acts to themselves and those around them. But why?

We all have unsettling feelings within us. Consider the last time you were angry at a co-worker or succeeded when someone said that you could not. The desire to dominate or humiliate another person is often at the back of our minds. The difference between ourselves and psychopaths is our decisions to act or dwell on unpleasant thoughts. To 99.99% of the population, it is unsettling to believe that anyone could act in violent or destructive ways.

Before the birth of psychology, people who exhibited strange or abusive behavior were confined to the realms of imagination. Werewolves, vampires, witches, and creatures in the woods were the only beings that would stoop to harming another. It was nearly impossible to believe that people could be responsible for killing again and again. When psychotic people were caught, they were confined to prisons, subjected to exorcisms, and sometimes killed for their involvement in heinous crimes.

Today, however, those acting on dark thoughts have a much greater platform in which to work. The term "iPredator," coined by Doctor of Psychology Micheal Nuccitelli, explains the predatory nature of people online. iPredators look for ways to accost people online, regardless of the feelings of others. Consider, for instance, cyberbullies. They are prevalent on the internet because it is so much easier to be anonymous, negating the effects of responsibility for negative actions. Often, more than one successful attempt to belittle another leads to more practiced forms of manipulation in the future.

Humans are the only creatures that express the need to dominate others unnecessarily. Dogs create a hierarchy for survival, but when all their needs are met—when they are living in caring, plentiful homes—they do not need the primitive necessity to control those under the alpha, which is why there are fewer fights than in the wild. All animals use dominance as a form of survival, except humans.

Social, racial, and cultural eradication is not uncommon in human history. The Nazis annihilated millions of Jewish people as a form of ethnic cleansing. Biblical Isrealites eradicated civilizations to take over land after leaving Egypt. In the 1990s, the Hutu—located in Rwanda—massacred hundreds of thousands of people, most of them Tutsies. The Soviet Union slaughtered millions of their own people in the name of Communism. The common theme in all of these examples is the necessity to manipulate others.

Most people have a reason for erratic and disturbing behavior. For example, in the arsonist's case, starting fires has little to do with the need to hurt others. In fact, they often suffer from past sexual abuses, and fires give them sexual arousal. Necrophiliacs often experience a need for control over others, which is why they turn to the dead for sexual gratification. They may not have control over their own relationships, so they seek objects that cannot resist.

Psychopathy

Serial killers often feel gratification when hurting others. Dark psychology suggests brutality in the forms of rape, torture, and murder are the only ways for truly psychotic people to feel a "rush." Psychopaths often do not feel strong emotions, which leads them to crime. Escalated crime gives them a chance to feel something. Psychopaths also often torture victims before murdering them to receive an extra thrill.

Psychopaths were labeled as sociopaths for many years, and many continue to use this term to describe the nature of people who act remorselessly. However, sociopathy refers to the effects of society on a mentally disturbed individual. Psychopaths have recently been proven to be in a category of their own. They are hardly affected by their surroundings, but instead possess an innate lack of empathy for others. Psychopaths like Ted Bundy were raised in good homes and did not lack for basic life necessities, but still killed for seemingly no reason.

Psychopaths in prison show no direct correlation between drug usage and psychopathic actions. Less than 50% of all psychopaths in prison have a reliance on drugs. Tempers are always close to the surface, and psychopathic serial killers often murder because someone "pushed my buttons."

Their highly parasitic natures often cause them to believe they are always connected with family and friends, when in fact, they are often avoided. They are also able to charm others into believing they are not monsters. It is common for first offender psychopaths to be released early due to good behavior. However, when released, they return to the same habits, once again seeking thrills.

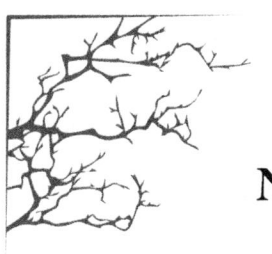

Narcissism

Narcissists are known to have grandiose thoughts and egotistic views, but there is more to it than that. Narcissists are also known for their lack of empathy, which usually manifests itself through toxic relationships, volatility, low self-esteem, and attention- seeking behaviors, just to name a few. They are known to make suicide attempts as a result of difficult situations, like losing a job or relationship. These suicide attempts are often dangerous, but non-lethal. They are mostly used to seek attention.

A narcissistic person, for example, may constantly complain of illness and show some symptoms, but disregard medical advice from others, claiming they received better help elsewhere. They may scream once behind locked doors, claiming that someone of the opposite sex offered unwanted sexual advanced. They might also call doctors in a panic, explaining small changes in physical or behavioral characteristics. Anything that warrants attention is fair game to a narcissist.

Narcissists were frequently classified under the Borderline Personality Disorder umbrella because of their difficulty deciphering emotions and thoughts. However, when tested with brain scans, it was determined that, though narcissists showed little to no physical connection with others regarding their emotions, their brains exhibited large fluctuations. Narcissists, therefore, have subconscious mind reading abilities that guide their actions.

Narcissists use unconscious information to manipulate others into doing what they want. For example, a narcissist will threaten suicide if a significant other tries to leave, perhaps even taking some steps toward suicide. They prey upon the empathy of others to fulfill their wishes.

Machiavellianism

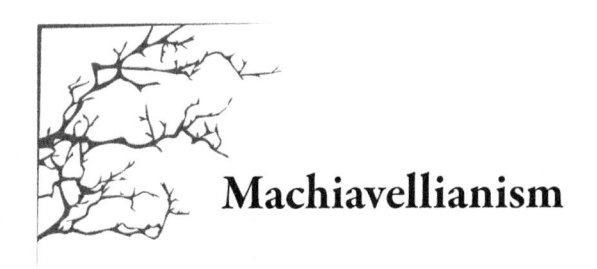

Machiavellians take advantage of the people around them by promoting their own ambitions on others. The term "Machiavellianism" was coined in the 1970s, but it has a much older history. Niccolo Machiavelli was primarily a philosopher and diplomat, but his book *Il Principe* ("The Prince") became renowned for its harsh views on the working class. His book illustrated the need for rulers and other high-ranking officials to use brutality as a source of motivation for their needs. Glory and honor were preferred over human life. Hence, those with Machiavellianism use and manipulate others for their ultimate benefits.

Machiavellians are often charming at first, which gets their feet in the door to exploit others in the future. However, they lack the empathy to care about those who have helped them in the past. Money and power are the most important things to Machiavellians, and they will lie, cheat, and steal to get what they want. Though they are skilled at reading people, they lack common social skills, often making them distant. Like psychopaths and narcissists, they often have troubles discerning their emotions, and they are unlikely to notice the negative repercussions of their actions.

If you are in a difficult law battle, consider hiring a Machiavellian. There is a reason most lawyers are considered bloodsucking vultures. Many are highly motivated to giving you the best outcome possible because they are highly motivated by power and money. They are eager to debate, which makes them excellent and some of the most sought-after lawyers.

Perhaps one of the most famous Machievellians in history was Joseph Stalin. Though he started out in a poor home, he rose through the ranks of the Communist party, ensuring that every major authority owed him their seat. He overthrew Vladimir Lenin's seat and instituted Communism. As a result, he reduced all Russians to menial workers, and many died due to forced labor and poor nutrition. He did not improve the state of the country to save the peoples' lives, causing the deaths of nearly 20 million people in one of the greatest acts of genocide of all time.

The Dark Triad

The term "dark triad" refers to the people who test positively for narcissism, psychopathy, and machiavellism. Consider these people to be the Voldemorts of the psychological world. They care little about others' emotions, and they mostly focus on themselves to gain power, money, and sometimes fame.

Members of the dark triad have antisocial behaviors. They rely on manipulation to make people do what they want, sometimes resorting to violence or abusive tendencies. They lack the ability to connect with others through trust, kindness, modesty, and straightforwardness.

Machiavellians and psychopaths are more likely to cheat than narcissists, but they all cheat in greater quantities than average. Narcissists mostly feel the need to cheat due to feelings of inadequacy, while Machiavellians and psychopaths do it when convenient. Again, narcissists differ from Machiavellians and psychopaths because they self-deceive, often without conscious knowledge.

All that test positive for dark triad characteristics show aggressive behavior. They are more likely to live erratically, taking part in bizarre sexual practices, bullying, and sexual harassment. They are also prone to mental illnesses such as depression and anxiety. People of the dark triad also commonly have genetic abnormalities, such as higher testosterone in men.

Of course, when reviewing narcissism, psychopathy, and Machiavellism, it is easy to believe you carry the same characteristics, pronouncing yourself a lost cause. Though there are tests that help you determine if you have these traits, the results are highly subjective. So, before you give up on yourself completely, know that only 0.01% of the population has these problems.

Manipulation

Predatory nature lies in all of us, which comes from the very beginning. Our first ancestors had to rely on instincts to eat, drink, and obtain shelter. As technology improved, so did civilization. Today, food comes from grocery stores, and use of the mind is more prevalent for attaining the necessities of life. Still, we use predatory instincts to manipulate those around us.

Manipulation comes in two forms: global and ordinary. Global manipulation dictates the thought processes of another, often taking over another's ability to think or act for themselves. For example, a global manipulator may include a psychopathic abductor who keeps children in the basement and forces them to believe one way or another by inflicting pain when they give an answer unsatisfactory to the abductor.

An ordinary manipulator, on the other hand, changes the way the recipient thinks through subliminal messaging. For example, Sydney may attempt to manipulate Daniel into doing something for her by using a variety of techniques, some of which are included below:

1. Sydney charms Daniel into buying her flowers by offering a kiss.
2. Sydney makes Daniel feel guilty for not buying her a new coat by giving passive-aggressive answers to

Daniel's questions.
3. Sydney withholds kindness when Daniel does not do the dishes.
4. Sydney makes Daniel believe she will be held in higher regard by her friends if she does him a favor.
5. Sydney makes Daniel doubt his monetary reality by insisting something only costs a small price.

These small acts of manipulation range from simple to extreme. Manipulation is often defined as "a form of influence that is neither coercion nor rational persuasion" (Stanford Encyclopedia of Philosophy, 2018). So, manipulation often illogically persuades someone to think contrary to their natural instincts. However, not all manipulation is bad. Subliminal messages in the world today are commonly used as nudges to make you think a certain way.

A common form of manipulation is marketing. A marketer for a mattress company does not force you to buy a mattress, but gently nudges you toward the idea. Tactics such as lowering prices, using bright colors, and using catchy phrases often lead customers to the store without even realizing it.

Grocery stores also use manipulation tactics to get you to buy more. More obvious persuasions like putting drinks and candy in the checkout lines are what most people think of when they think of grocery store manipulation, but they are far from the only tactics. Fruit is often displayed at the entrance of the store because the bright colors exude freshness and make you more excited. Milk and eggs are located at the back of the store to make you walk through isles of products to reach those relatively common products. Merchandise with expiration dates often last longer than their dates suggest. Studies even reach neurological methods, using MRIs to calculate how much pleasure certain products bring and placing those items in strategic places.

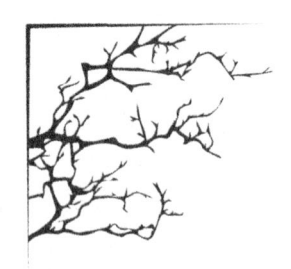

Sleight of Hand

M any believe that voodoo, witchcraft, or demonic persuasion exists, and not just in the sense that there are curses placed. However, there are some people who can perform magnificent stunts seemingly by magic. Where do you fit in this?

People who delve into magic often use the power of suggestion and sleight of hand to change the laws of nature. If you have been to Las Vegas or seen pictures of street performers, you may be familiar with levitation. Performers on the street sit, seemingly suspended in air, over a rug or blanket, held in place only by holding onto a cane. These magicians can suspend in air for hours, not moving, lifted only by the power in their hands.

David Copperfield made history when he made the Statue of Liberty disappear. He gathered his audience at a site close to the State of Liberty and lifted a curtain in front of the monument for a few moments. When the curtain was removed, the Statue of Liberty had simply disappeared.

Sleight of hand is simply manipulation. You are tricking your audience into thinking they see something they do not, or nothing at all. When a magician performs a card trick, they draw most of the attention to a moving hand, while the other moves quickly to complete the trick. By drawing attention to objects or gestures, they make you see the unimaginable.

Deception of the Mind

Even though it may seem like we understand everything we see, it is often confused by things it does not understand. It tries to explain what the eyes bring in by characterizing the image with something it already knows. For example, picture an image in which the houses appear slanted sideways. There are also trees, shrubs, and a mail vehicle, which also give the illusion that the architects were slightly tipsy when designing this layout. However, when you tilt your screen or view, the houses are actually straight while everything else is slightly slanted.

Why, then, does it first look like the houses are slanted? Your brain immediately interprets what you see in the image. Since everything in the image is relatively straight except for the houses, your brain interprets the picture accordingly. For most people, it takes a few seconds to correctly interpret this image.

Everything that comes through our eyes is upside-down. Our brains take the information retrieved from the eyes and try to make sense of the images. The mind requires its own rules for separating images, prioritizing some aspects over others. Trying to rewire your brain to see something differently is often very difficult and takes time and practice.

To test how your mind works, consider words that are written in another color that what they are. For example, you'd have green (written in blue), yellow (written in red), red (written in orange), orange (written in pink), green (written in yellow), blue (written in green), black (written in pink), and so on. Imagine first reading every word, then reading every color of each word.

GREEN - YELLOW - RED - ORANGE - - BLUE - BLACK - PURPLE - BLUE - ORANGE - BLACK -

If you are like most people, it is easier for you to read the words instead of the colors. Your mind takes preference reading the words instead of the colors, and forcing your mind to see the colors is often difficult.

Conditioning others to feel differently is another form of mind deception that makes others believe you have a sixth sense. Considering trying this exercise with two friends: Have both of your friends stand facing each other, more than two arm-distances away. Have friend one close their eyes and raise

SUGGESTION: SECRETS OF COVERT MANIPULATION

their right arm. Friend two should also raise their right arm, but their eyes need not close. Carefully, wave your arms above and below friend one's extended arm to show there are no strings connecting the two. Then, stroke friend two's extended arm. If done properly, friend one should feel the brush of the arm, exactly where friend two's arm was stroked.

The power of suggestion will make friend one feel the brush stroke from friend two. Why? There are a couple of reasons for this. Once the eyes are closed, the body focuses on different senses. It is likely that friend one heard the rustle of your waving arms or the feel of a slight breeze across their forearms. The second is due to neural impulses in the brain.

Have you ever experienced that prickly feeling in the back of your neck like someone was staring at you when you were engrossed in something else, like sending a text or reading a book? The mind can detect small changes in body motion just by cellular reactions. These reactions occur all over your body, making you hyper-aware of your surroundings.

The brain reacts to suggested results. When your body expects an outcome, it will conceive of a way to make it happen. Placebos in medical experiments are more or less sugar pills. They do nothing for the body, but the mind suggests the pill makes some difference. In fact, placebos may help hypochondriacs feel better. The suggestion by a certified professional that the pills do something is often enough to assure those convinced of a false terminal illness they will be saved. Brain trickery is one of the best ways to deceive others, and the power of persuasion is often irreplaceable in the art of deception.

What to Expect

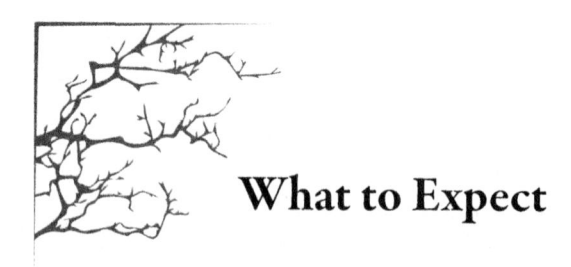

The art of manipulation is not an absolute science, but you can hone your skills. This book gives you the tools to gently persuade others to do and believe what you want. As with every other art form, practice is key.

Many who read this book want to change the suggestions and lives of those around them. Everyone can get something from this book. Spouses often find the methods of persuasion helpful to enhance their relationships by gently manipulating a husband or wife to see them in a different light or to treat them differently. Lonely people often use manipulation to develop relationships with friends and partners. Salespeople find manipulation one of their best tools to ensure the sales of their items. Attorneys use persuasion tactics to make juries believe in a client. Leaders can make employees work harder through perceived good graces or charms.

Many people use dark psychology to get what they want. Often, they resort to withholding affection or praise, lying, and reverse psychology. Salespeople often use fearmongering or choice restriction to get customers to buy products they sell. There is a fine line between persuading someone and bullying them into a decision.

It is easy to fall into the trap of believing you must use tactics from the dark triad to get your way, but there are more ethi-

SUGGESTION: SECRETS OF COVERT MANIPULATION

cal ways to persuade people to believe what you want. Discover what your tactics are to persuade people in your life. Do not resort to harmful tactics to get what you want. Avoid all-or-nothing conversations. Instead, make others comfortable by using creative deception of mind to give them what they want.

Chapter 2: Know Thyself and Modify Thy Behavior

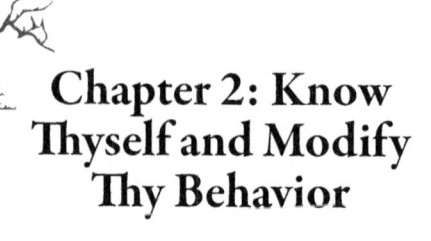

"Knowing others is intelligence; knowing yourself is true wisdom. Mastering others is strength; mastering yourself is true power. If you realize that you have enough, you are truly rich."

- *Lao Tzu*

The first step to understanding others is to know yourself. Consider how you behave when something happens to you. Are you easily riled when someone disagrees with you, or do you find yourself silently fuming? Are you happy for a friend when they earn an achievement, or are you secretly jealous of their good fortune?

The way you know yourself and behave is the beginning of good persuasion. Think about it. When playing poker, the tells and rituals many have determines how good their hand is. Wiping a finger under a nose or meticulously shifting the cards in your hands can determine if you are bluffing or not. If people cannot tell what you are thinking when you are persuading them, you are more likely to manipulate others better.

Of course, the only way to understand others' behavior is to understand your own. The human experience is individual. Everyone has buttons to push and pictures that make them cry.

The psychology of the soul lets you understand what you are like, allowing you to project onto others.

Know Yourself

Teenagers often feel lost growing up, not knowing who they truly are, which often leads to experimentation. Gothic makeup and dress often help teenagers feel unique and deep. Popular teenagers often use their friends to find themselves by mimicking personalities or developing trends. Scholastic teenagers spend their time in books and bookish activities, finding out who they are by studying others.

However, knowing yourself is not limited to your teenage years. On the contrary, many try to find themselves for years and occasionally completely change course when they feel unsatisfied. Finding yourself is part of life, and no one ever feels like they have everything figured out. Knowing yourself is about focusing on yourself and living life intentionally.

Self-Transparency and Introspection

To know yourself, you must experience self-transparency and introspection. Both of these terms fall under the self-knowledge umbrella but have slightly different meanings. Where introspection means looking at your inward self, self-transparency is commonly associated with what you project to the world. Therefore, to know who you are on the inside involves looking outward.

Introspection expresses the way you think. It was John Locke who stated, "[It is] impossible for any one to perceive, without perceiving that he does perceive. When we see, hear, smell, taste, feel, meditate, or will anything, we know that we do so," (as quoted from Gertler, 2020). So, when we observe something, it is impossible to not acknowledge that we are observing. For example, think about the chair you are sitting in. You may acknowledge the sensations you feel as your arms brush the seat or how your backside feels against the material. Once you start to observe these sensations, your brain then acknowledges that you are thinking about it.

Introspection also requires inner thought related to oneself. Think about the condition of your brain, the way your body operates. However, to achieve true introspection, you must discover who you are from what you think only. Many people alter this step by reflecting on what others have said about them. But, introspection is highly personal. There is a reason that Henry Thoreau went into the woods for solitude for over two years. He eliminated all distractions and wrote *Walden*, believing that the hustle and bustle of interaction with others can remove you from yourself.

Be observant, too, of your current mental state. If you feel disappointed in a friend or family member, acknowledge that your disappointment generates from another's actions. Simply put, you can understand your mental state by observing where your emotions come from. Your disappointment is temporary and does not have an overarching effect on your mental state. Your current mental state may be one of stress or depression, happiness or anticipation. Honing the ability to understand your current mental state will help you understand others' as well.

So, how does introspection help you know yourself? In most cases, people do not know why they behave in certain ways. In fact, many have not even used introspection techniques in the past, making thoughts about their actions seem foreign. Why, for example, do you always yell at the barking dog in the middle of the night? Sure, it may be annoying, but there is more to it than that. You are expressing frustration and anger due to the effect of the noise on your sleeping habits. You may feel annoyed because you have your own dog and know how to properly discipline it, directing your anger at your neighbor instead.

An experiment conducted by Richard Nisbett and Nancy Bellows in 1977 determined how both introspective and non-introspective factors played into judging someone else. Participants were asked to interview others given a list of questions. The participants then told Nisbett and Bellows their assessments of the interviewee's answers, which required introspection.

However, participants also mentioned other variables that had nothing to do with the questions. Some of the interviewees spilled coffee or had a quirk that had a profound effect on some of the participants. They noted an interviewee's compassion by the way they responded to the distractions. In the end, both Nisbett and Bellows concluded that people generally judge others based on their own experiences.

Actions are often harder to explain when they are associated with attitudes. For example, people who are racist claim they are not to not appear in negative lights. However, when paired with someone of another color, they often display expressions of disgust and drift toward people of their own race. Their attitude, whether founded inside or outside the home, was determined through no additional thought. Therefore, when confronted, they do not acknowledge the look given.

When asked why they feel a certain way about a person or object, many quickly attach an emotion to it. To illustrate, imagine a picture of a chicken. What is the first thing that comes to your mind? Take a few moments to close your eyes and think about the picture. Without looking at it again, explain what the picture makes you feel. What object do you associate with the chicken? How did you come to that conclusion?

Most people do not know exactly how they came to that conclusion. You may have assigned a reason for why you feel a certain way, but you have likely never had to think about it before. Your attitude toward the chicken influenced your depiction of the image. For instance, you may have associated the chicken with a farm, small towns, a pitchfork, or a falling sky. When asked about why they associated their word with this picture, most will confabulate a story. In other words, the mind comes up with strange and unusual associations to make the connection. Introspection of attitude is very difficult to differentiate.

Attitude is exceptionally easy to manipulate. In a study conducted by Daniel Wegner, participants were asked to look at faces of the opposite sex and to explain which was the most attractive. As a twist to the study, when he had finished showing the faces, Wegner held up a different face than the participants had described. Only 28% of the participants noticed the difference. When asked why they were attracted to the different picture, they expressed features that were different from their original choice. For example, one man explained he had chosen the wrong picture because he liked blonds, when in reality, he had chosen a woman with brown hair (Schwitzgebel, 2019).

On the other hand, actually *thinking* of how you came to a conclusion is much easier to track in your mind. For instance, find x in the equation $2x + 2 = 4$. When completed, explain how you got that answer. You should have a definitive list of steps you took to get to that conclusion. Thinking about why you go through the motions of daily life, therefore, is much easier than explaining sensations.

Attitudes and feelings are much easier to manipulate, so understanding why you behave the way you do gives you a clue of why others behave the way they will. You can change a person's perspective on marriage by associating negative reactions with positive images. You can manipulate a child into studying by rewarding behavior for hard work. The images they associate with actions will change others' behavior without detection.

Living Intentionally

Our days are filled with small actions, many of them unintentional. The simplicity of modern life has made much of it automatic. Small choices like purchasing a jacket online with fast delivery and one click of a button is easy, and it often does not cross your mind how much money you spend. Telling someone a little white lie often does not pull on any morality strings. Giving someone an unwitting glance may not seem like much, but they may interpret it negatively (or too positively).

Not many people think about what they do today. With busy schedules, it is easy to dissolve into the anxieties and pressures of modern life. However, if you stop to notice what is going on around you as you ride the subway or sit at home, you may realize yourself becoming more aware of not only your surroundings but of yourself as well.

The first step in living intentionally is to give yourself at least five minutes of quiet reflection. Whether that means you can connect with nature or have to barricade yourself in the bathroom, give yourself the time with as few distractions as possible at the beginning of your day. With eyes closed, imagine your perfect day. Are you spending most of it with friends and family? Are you going to work or spending your time creating? Are you at peace, or do you find stressors creeping in?

SUGGESTION: SECRETS OF COVERT MANIPULATION

Discover your priorities and develop time for yourself in the future to consider how your priorities change.

Start to ask yourself deep-ended questions, like *What do I find inspiring? How do I spend my time?* or *How can I set my passions on fire?* These types of questions help you recognize what means the most to you. You should not be a slave to circumstance. The mind is often on autopilot because it is easier than constantly thinking about your actions. Ask yourself these questions when by yourself or throughout the day when you have nothing else to think about.

Do not show judgement for your answers. It is easy to get caught in a cycle of blaming ourselves for how we think. You may feel amused or confused at what you find, but it is simply your mind telling you some truth about yourself you may not have had time to consider. Remember, nothing is too extreme. Shutting your thoughts down as you experience them will prevent you from understanding yourself. Have some fun with the answers to find your true passions.

Writing down your thoughts lets you explore them later. If you do not have a lot of time to meditate, you may want to think about what you wrote down later. Whether you are a stay-at-home parent or work long hours, there are always points in the day to think about what you wrote down. You might find that the time you take to think about what you wrote down may be the most relaxing thoughts of the day.

Next, develop a small list of tasks to do in the morning. It can be as simple as preparing a smoothie for breakfast or as difficult as getting your kids ready for school. The list you create will remind you to think about your actions. As soon as you have mastered the list in the morning, move on to the afternoon and evening.

Many get caught up in the many tasks they have to complete throughout the day. If you list every small action you perform, your list will easily reach 10 pages, so instead of writing down your bathroom breaks, just be conscious of your actions. Once you make this a daily habit, it becomes easier.

If you become anxious by analyzing your every step, take a moment to stop and breathe. We breathe unconsciously but focusing on it for several minutes throughout the day will help you relax. When manipulating others, it is important to breathe consciously before completing actions. If you slow down enough, you can deceive anyone. People who consciously breathe can regulate their heart rates and maintain straight faces. All it requires is mindfully slowing your breath and finding your center.

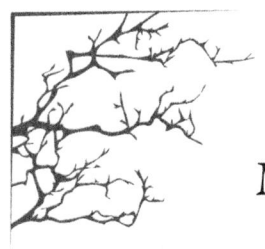

Meditation

Make a habit of meditating every day. Mindfulness helps your brain heal from stresses and focuses your life on the positive moments and successes in your life. Living intentionally also aids in physical health. If you have ever had a panic attack, you know that sometimes the best solution is to take several deep breaths to let your body calm down. It also often helps your body lower blood pressure, improve sleep, and aid heart disease. Even without the benefits of understanding others, mindfulness and meditation has a profound influence for good.

Meditation is about connecting your mind with your body, understanding who you are through observation. Consider this method for meditation when you begin your mindfulness practices. Practice it daily for at least five minutes.

As you sit or lie down, close your eyes and take deep breaths. Feel your breath enter your body through your mouth, then your throat, then into your lungs. You may feel your stomach also rise and fall as you continue to breathe at a steady pace. The next breath you take in, imagine the air reaching all the way through your body to your toes. As you exhale, imagine negative energy leaving your body, and continue to exhale until there is no more breath in your lungs. Return to a steady breathing cycle as you feel the energy of your body come in through your breath, the negative energy leaving your body with each exhale.

Next, become aware of the different parts of your body. First, recognize how your feet feel as they rest on a surface. Move on to your calves as you take steady breaths in and out. Feel the way your thighs connect with the rest of your body and the surface on which you are sitting. Recognize the muscles in your glutes and how they feel as you breathe in positive energy. Move up to your abdomen and feel the breath that comes in your body makes it slowly rise and fall. Feel your chest, your lungs, and heart moving together to make your body flow evenly. Then, move to your throat and head; recognize the muscles in your face and force them to relax.

As you come out of your meditative state, slowly open your eyes and take one final breath of positive energy. Exhale to let go of your stressors, anxieties, and negative thoughts. Since you are now more aware of your body, take the time to take stock of your ideas and value what you find.

Modify Your Behavior

Have you ever seen arguments played out on social media? In many cases, both sides yell at each other, neither of them convincing the other of their way. Instead, both sides are stuck in an endless loop of debate, further cementing themselves in their own beliefs. So, it should make sense that you need to modify your behavior to manipulate them. After all, how you manipulate someone is ultimately a reflection of who they are.

The Science-Based Principles to Behavior Modification

People act according to their feelings, their guts, their passions, making it difficult to pinpoint exact methods to change their behavior. However, everyone acts relatively the same way to the same stimuli. For example, it is a natural impulse to feel angry at inconveniences. It is natural to feel happy when something works out in your favor. It is natural to feel sad when a loved one dies.

True manipulators can see these changes in behavior and mimic them, making their reactions to stimuli seem natural. Naturally, if a friend is feeling happy about getting a promotion at their job, you would feel happy for them. They expect you to react in a supporting role. Reacting contrarily to their expectations creates a barrier between you and your friend. Even if you feel jealous for their promotion, increasing your attention to the emotions you show can influence them to act according to your gain, giving you a free dinner if done correctly. Below are the principles in behavior modification.

1. Reciprocation

When someone gives you a gift, it is polite to thank them in return, but it is more common to give a gift in return. After all, people are more likely to give something to you in response to a gift given. Likewise, if you do someone a favor, they are more likely to do you a favor in the future.

One of the most common examples of reciprocity is in restaurants. It is customary to give servers tips for their work, and their tips reflect how they treated you. However, several studies have uncovered an increase in tips after giving small gifts to the customer after meals, such as mints. When a single mint was given to customers after eating, tips raised 3%. When given two mints, the gratuity increased by 14%. When the server gave each customer a mint, walked away, paused, then turned back and said something like, "for you nice people, I want to give you one more," the gratuity increased a whopping 23% (Cialdini, 2019).

Reciprocity, then, is not just about the giving of gifts, but the way you give them. Servers who behaved kindly toward customers received an increase of tips, but their method of kindness also had a profound impact. Customers believed the servers were giving them preferential treatment, persuading them to give more. If you offer to help someone move, you are more likely to receive a bigger favor than if they approached you. The attitudes you display are some of your most important skills in persuasion.

1. Commitment and Consistency

When you make a commitment with someone and fail to follow through, you lose credibility. For example, if you plan to spend a weekend with a friend, following through will persuade them to invite you to more events in the future. If you keep up this behavior, your friend becomes more susceptible to your influence.

Doctors have found that people who write down their own follow-up dates are more likely to remember them than those who received a call or have the appointment written down for them. Written, contractual evidence is harder to forget. That is also why students who write notes on paper are more likely to do well in tests than those who either recorded the lectures or typed them down on a laptop.

Try, for example, asking your friend to join you for a night out. If they return the same old rhetoric of refusal due to some fabricated excuse, go a little further. Assert that they should come because they owe you loyalty. When they finally consent, thank them for their commitment and instill a sense of expectation in the future.

1. Social Proof

People like proof, and it is usually best from other people. This is why employers ask for references and online shoppers look at reviews of products before they buy them. It is one thing for you to pronounce your excellence to the world, but it is quite another when someone else endorses you.

One of the most common examples of social proof is social media influencers. Influencers like Kylie Jenner or the Daily Dose channel can endorse or forgo representation of companies and products, and others will buy according to what these influencers say. They have created such a following that millions may respond to whatever they say.

Hotels have also conducted studies regarding social proof. These studies have revealed that 75% of people in hotels reuse towels previously used. So, to influence others to reuse their towels more often, they left a note telling hotel guests of these findings and encouraging others to do the same to help the environment. Adding a quip about the environment encouraged an additional 28% of those not reusing towels to reuse them, where adding nothing about this did not provide the same results.

1. Liking

It is much easier to get others to do something for you if they like you. People are not looking for people who are simply attractive, intelligent, or athletic for likeability, either. The most common traits of likeability are transparency, honesty, and trustworthiness. When people act sincerely, they are better able to manipulate others.

Likeable people are interested in what you say. Have you ever spent time with someone who listened to you? When they listened to your problems, your interests, or your life, talking became easier. Listening plays another role in manipulation. If you listen to what other people say, it becomes easier to develop strategies to manipulate them. For example, some people are highly socially inept. When they find someone who will listen to them and be their friend, they cling to what makes them feel safe. You can capitalize on this by making them do favors for you, forcing tests of their loyalty.

Likeable people also do not pass judgements. They let others be the spotlights of their own lives. These people look for ways to help other people. If you feel uncomfortable with exploiting your friends to practice your manipulation, use likeability to encourage others to do things for you without saying a word. Some people are so likeable that doing something for them makes you feel good.

In a study done with business students at two universities, they were asked to complete a business plan with which everyone could agree. The first university simply said, "time is money, so begin." The second university asked the students to first get to know each other. By the end of the time allotted, only 55% of the university students agreed. The second university, however, boasted an impressive 90% agreement after the time given. After just a few minutes of getting to know each other, these students gained likeability and could agree on a business plan.

1. Authority

People respond to those who know what they are talking about or appear to have some authority. Think of the last time you went to the grocery store. Asking one of the workers with a uniform is more helpful than asking someone who has shopped in that grocery store for years.

Therapists and doctors also use this method to acquire new patients. Physicians and psychotherapists with displayed diplomas are more likely to see improvements in their number of appointments than those who do not. Likewise, people who dress in work-appropriate attire are considered of higher substance.

Dressing appropriately works both ways. Studies have shown that dressing in attire that fits the job encourages you to work harder. Dressing appropriately and exuding confidence are two of the most important ways to increase a sense of authority.

Authority is also enhanced by others' endorsements as well. While you may find some success bragging about your skills, people are more eager to work with you if someone else has advocated for you. Real estate companies use this method often to get more customers. When calling the office, other employees endorse the merits of coworkers by giving their accreditations. Someone calling for buying property on the south side of town may be directed to someone who has 15 years of experience in the area. Studies have shown that endorsing others has led to a 20% rise in leads.

1. Scarcity

The principle of scarcity coerces people into believing that a service or product is rare or limited, forcing them to act now. Jewelers have perpetuated this lie for years in the form of selling diamonds. Diamonds are actually fairly common, with some scientists estimating the number of tons in the quadrillions. Why, then, is purchasing a diamond so expensive? Marketers have convinced people that diamonds are rare, and therefore, valuable. Most jewelers pay far less for their diamonds than they sell them for.

People are more drawn to things that are stated to be rare or unique, even if they are not. Offering services for a limited time may drive sales if done properly. Many online courses use language like, "The value of this course is $1,000, but it is now

SUGGESTION: SECRETS OF COVERT MANIPULATION

on sale for only $100!" or "Only the first 100 who apply to this amazing deal will receive an extra gift!" The tantalizing idea of "it is now or never" allows you to easily manipulate people who do not do their research.

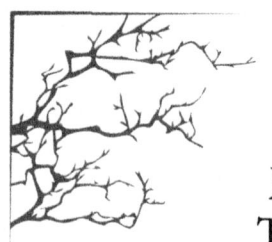

Mastering Techniques

Now that you know the principles for basic manipulation, it is time to delve into modifying your behavior through practice. No one is a master at manipulation at the start. Though some children seem to have the behavior down to a science, it may have taken years for them to condition parents into giving them what they want. Everyone has to start from somewhere.

Many famous manipulators have used outside resources or their own skills to influence others. The most famous dictators in history developed a skill and continued to use it to influence the masses. It seems impossible for many to be convinced that horrendous actions are necessary, but great manipulators can make it happen.

Adolf Hitler convinced his people that the Germans were fighting for the right cause in World War II because of his great speeches. Listeners often commented that he had the ability to read the air of the people and speak from the heart. In most cases, he convinced people that they already agreed with what he taught. His first attack on Munich failed miserably, but using his power of speech, he soon gained a larger audience.

Joseph Stalin used propaganda to push his agenda and convince others that he was the most important man in history.

SUGGESTION: SECRETS OF COVERT MANIPULATION

Though he did also lead through fear, he maintained his position at the top by inserting himself into history books and renaming cities after himself to convince others of his greatness.

Fidel Castro convinced his own people that the torture they were enduring was based on good intentions. He started his regime with failed coups and guerilla warfare, but he eventually pushed communism on his people. He created a plan to limit foreign ownership, seemingly to bring independence back to rural farmers, but this caused problems with foreign companies and took the land for the state instead. He also tried to unite countries through brutal communism, encouraging countries to fight instead of use peaceful tactics.

All of these masters of manipulation stayed in power as long as they did because they were excellent at the skills they practiced. They recognized how they could improve their skills to influence others and eventually persuaded people, en masse, to follow them.

Though these dark examples do not have to be your influences for using manipulation, they offer examples of how much you can influence others by practicing your skills. Some of the best ways to improve your natural talents are both easy and cheap, and you can work on them in your spare time.

1. Take an Acting Class

Acting classes let you explore your own creativity. They also teach you how to behave around others. A common method of acting is mirroring. It teaches you to control your emotions by exhibiting the emotions and actions of another. To mirror accurately, you must build a connection with them by making eye contact. Make them the new center of focus, ignoring distractions and pretend that they are the most important person in your universe. Follow their every move, down to the pace of their movements. Notice every quirk that they do and copy it.

Another style of acting is method acting. Method acting is all internal: it is about putting your body in place of another's. Use their actions and movements as inspiration for your own, falling into a type of meditation to reach this state. Use your own emotional background to influence your performance as another person. The final step is to become your character. If you want to manipulate a coworker, pick up their mannerisms and speech patterns. Become who they are when they are not looking.

1. Work on Charisma

Linking back to the likeability principle, charisma is the ability to charm others. Charismatic people light up a room when they walk in, and truly charming people can manipulate you into doing something with a smile. The key to a charismatic performance is genuinity. Be present for the person you are trying to charm by actively listening, making them feel important.

Make yourself appear physically comfortable by uncrossing your arms and not fidgeting. If you are constantly worried about how your clothes are making your body look, you cannot be physically present with another person. They will detect your discomfort and likely clam up. You can appear more comfortable by making eye contact, making others believe they are special. When making eye contact, you exude honesty, trust, and sincerity, traits most people search for in a companion.

SUGGESTION: SECRETS OF COVERT MANIPULATION

Make them comfortable by nodding frequently, and at the right time. Though a small motion, nodding gives the appearance of active listening. Nodding shows the other person you agree with what they have to say, bonding you closer to them. Ask clarifying questions to show them you are engaged with their conversation. Most people will break down walls when they know someone else is interested in them.

1. Take a Debate Class

Have you ever argued with someone only to realize your perfect comeback to a particularly vicious response did not come until the night after your argument? Taking a debate class helps you develop your thoughts appropriately, and in the right time. Debate is a common tool used by manipulators to either overwhelm or gently persuade their opponents. And true debaters know how to win arguments that will convince everyone their opinion is best.

The key rule to good debating is keeping calm. Those who remain calm do not appear to be driven by emotion. If you act emotionally, your opponent can make you appear irrational, making spectators reject your facts and opinions. Confidence in your opinions make you more agreeable. Most of your calm, confident persona is evident through your body language. Shoulders back, head up, and feet spread hip-width apart give you the illusion of dominance.

1. Learn from a Master

Master manipulators like Hans Scharff developed techniques to get information from others without their knowledge. Scharff was a German Luftwaffe interrogator who became known as one of the best interrogators in the world. Instead of using brutality, he treated his prisoners with respect and kindness, occasionally bringing them homemade goods to ensure their trust. He would then take prisoners on walks, asking only that they did not try to escape. During their walks, prisoners would often reveal secrets without realizing.

Master manipulators are great communicators. They charm people with their words, and they set others at ease with their actions. Often, master manipulators are calm and collected, appearing to own the room. They make friends easily, but many cannot keep them since they may turn sour at a moment's notice. They use sarcasm and the occasional glib comment.

They seek vulnerability while always playing the victim. Manipulators may go off topic to draw out someone's vulnerability while simultaneously condemning them. This form of manipulation is common on social media. For example, someone may disapprove of a celebrity's actions, and the manipulator will turn the argument to an issue of race or sexism. The manipulator always aims to make others believe they are the subject of ridicule, when in fact, they use passive aggressive methods to turn the minds of others.

A master manipulator will also never break character. They will stick to a story regardless of facts disputing otherwise. They will take chances to humiliate others to accomplish their own gains, making audiences believe they were attacked. Hot button terms are common ammunition for master manipulators, degrading another, especially when cornered. They develop a sense of teaming, forcing the audience to believe it is a fight for what is right. By studying these tactics, you can develop language that encourages others to take your side, referencing wrong-doings to advocate for their positions.

Chapter 3: Power Play: Know Thy Neighbor

"When you know what a man wants, you know who he is, and how to move him."

- J.R.R. Martin

The basis for any manipulation is understanding human nature. Taking the time to know yourself from the previous chapter should have highlighted this. Others can be easily manipulated if you play into their vulnerabilities, which often include taking advantage of their kindness, affection, and sense of morality. Manipulation often requires a strong stomach. For many, it is difficult to manipulate others because it requires a ruthless nature, capitalizing on others' faults to elevate yourself.

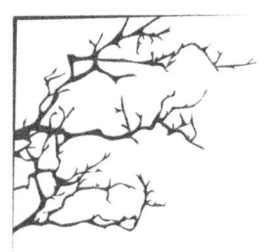

Morality

Most people pursue an innate sense of morality. The laws we follow are an essential part of morality, as they require the integrity of citizens to properly work. Good, law-abiding citizens do not need the punishment of jail to keep them from committing a felony since they have a conscious desire to adhere to laws.

One of the most debated topics, however, is the subject of internal morality, and whether it is present at birth or cultivated by the environment. You have surely heard of the phrase "nature or nurture" in the past. This simple phrase questions whether humans are naturally good or are raised to become good people. Is it the responsibility of the person to have their own moral compass, or is it the job of society to raise that child correctly?

The debate has continued for years with no definitive correct answer. Manipulators then use this to their advantages. They make others believe they were not raised correctly, had some sort of trauma in their pasts, or had some other disconnect from human interaction. This method often garners sympathy, which a master manipulator will use to their advantage.

Morality is important to manipulation because you can determine someone's actions based on their moral compass. True manipulators find the vulnerabilities in a person's morality and exploit them. After all, to manipulators, what most people would call virtues, they call weaknesses.

Manipulators see emotions as a chemical reaction in the brain that is a conditioned response to human life. Master manipulators believe emotions come from evolution instead of some innate moral compass. Suffering yields compassion in those unfamiliar with how to guide their feelings. The response has been conditioned because of our ancestors' need to stay in groups and protect the injured to survive. In essence, manipulators are cold and calculating, sacrificing the feelings of others to serve their purposes.

However, manipulation used for the benefit of others uses the same techniques. A therapist may manipulate their clients into caring for a child by playing on the client's natural tendency to care for others. A friend may counsel a neighbor to leaving an abusive relationship by changing their mind about affection.

Manipulation is about changing the way someone thinks, for good or bad. If you are looking to influence others to do good by using manipulative skills, you must not slip into moral gray areas. Telling an associate that their spouse is a rotten, stealing wretch delves into a dark gray area, using bullying instead of helpful persuasion to encourage change.

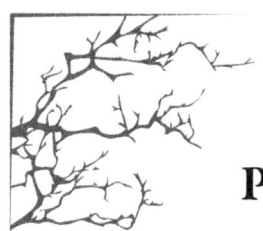

Personalities

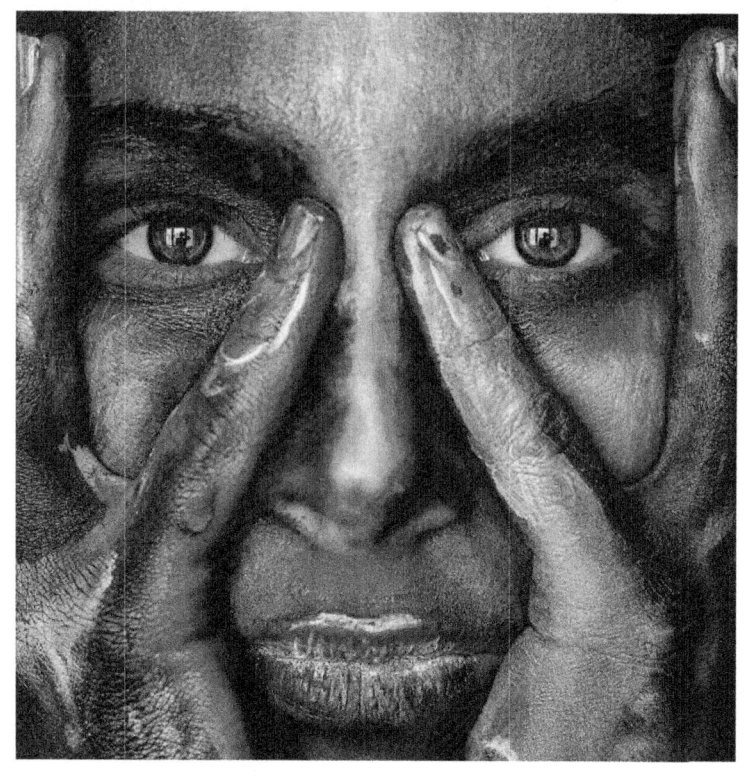

In the last chapter, you delved into your own thoughts and patterns, what makes you act the way you do. However, to manipulate someone, it takes more than understanding your own sets of morals and traits to manipulate the way someone thinks. For example, they may not be swayed by charms but are more impressed with social proofs. They may appear to be boisterous, but their mannerisms may prevent them from truly opening up to people.

To understand how a person ticks comes down to their personality traits. Though everyone is different, everyone contains a mixture of characteristics, commonly known as the big five personality traits. People with "large" personalities contain characteristics that are easily seen, while those on the quiet side usually hide their true personalities. Psychologists use personality traits to identify problems and provide answers, much like manipulators can.

Openness to Experience

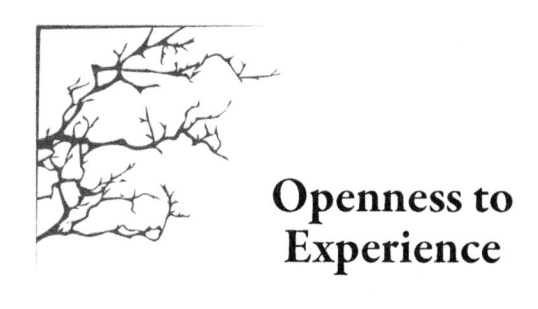

Openness to experience measures a person's willingness to try new things. More open people are more likely to travel and try new things. They often experiment with cultures and enjoy risks. They take opportunities and are more likely to accept different viewpoints. Closed people, however, are tucked further into their own shells. They prefer to stay in a lifestyle in which they are familiar. It is more comfortable for them to have a routine, and they are less likely to take risks.

Open people are often considered more intelligent than closed people simply because they are more likely to take chances. They show creativity and strive to learn. They are also more likely to adapt to various physical, mental, and emotional environments, seeing setbacks as challenges instead of obstacles.

Though openness changes throughout life, younger people are more likely to be open than older people. Women are also slightly more open than men, though both of these determinants vary with culture. Western culture is usually associated with a more open style, valuing individuality over the collective. However, people of all cultures exhibit signs of openness.

Manipulators find open people easier to persuade than closed people. Since open people are more likely to trust, charm and wit are commonly used to manipulate open people. Closed people are more easily manipulated through facts. Since they are less likely to leave their comfort zones, they usually require truly charismatic people to open them up. Less spontaneous, closed people require commitment and consistency, so they are often a project.

Agreeableness

Agreeable people are anxious to be part of society. They like to be involved with others and strive to be the peacemaker of the group. As such, they usually avoid confrontation, preferring harmony. Agreeable people are also very generous, thoughtful, and kind, eager to help people who are less fortunate. People who are not agreeable exhibit antisocial behavior. They are usually quite abrasive and start arguments. They find a thrill in making others feel inferior. They are often selfish and make others feel inferior.

Agreeable people are often less bullied than their less-agreeable counterparts. However, disagreeable people show bullying behavior, especially to cover inferiorities. Agreeable people are influenced by their environments. Though anyone can start off with an agreeable personality, studies have shown that people lower agreeableness when subjected to abusive behavior, just as anyone else would.

Disagreeable people are more commonly defined by dark psychology characteristics. That means that psychopaths, narcissists, and Machiavellians are more likely to be disagreeable than any other personality trait. With study, disagreeable people can mimic agreeable traits and use them to influence people.

Since likeability is the most basic principle associated with agreeableness, manipulators can use this to their advantage. Becoming likeable largely depends on appearing charming, which is an easily-learned trait. Manipulators can take advantage of an agreeable person's peacemaker qualities by threatening fights or playing on their unselfish natures.

Agreeableness is defined by social desirability. Often that means manipulators can play on social cues to persuade others in the form of peer pressure. Popularity is the measuring stick of agreeableness, and once an audience is captured, manipulators can easily influence them for good or bad. A master manipulator, for example, might encourage followers to treat targets as inferior if they do not comply with basic manipulator standards. On the other hand, manipulators can encourage masses to clean environments or donate to a worthy cause.

Extraversion and Introversion

You have likely heard of introverts and extroverts. After all, the world seems to divide people into these two categories as some of the largest personality traits. However, just like the other traits, introversion and extroversion are not black and white. They are extremes on a scale of attention. Psychologists use "introvert" and "extravert" tags to explain how people behave. Introverts prefer the company of a small group of friends, while an extravert (or extrovert) enjoys the company of anyone.

Extraverts are the life of the party and highly attention-seeking. They get their energy from social gatherings and rely on others to make them feel better. An extravert's behavior is dictated by the actions of others, while an introvert tends to find solace within. Introverts are generally considered more cerebral, since they like their own company to learn. They receive energy from connecting with themselves, spending quiet time to reflect.

Introverts and extraverts differ due to their cortical arousal, which refers to the stimulus given to the brain. Introverts have a naturally higher level of cortical arousal than extraverts, which means their minds are more easily stimulated. Extraverts require interactions with others to raise their cortical arousal, which is why many extraverts are more drawn to hobbies that include others.

It is highly debated whether introversion and extraversion are traits by nature or environment. Studies have shown that identical twins are more likely to share introverted or extraverted behavior than fraternal twins, which suggests there is a connection to genetics. However, siblings in the same family exhibit different levels on the introversion and extraversion scale, so it is hard to pinpoint the exact cause.

Manipulators who prey on extraverts often find success by forcing affection to limit social interactions. For example, a boyfriend may restrict how much his girlfriend can interact with her friends, threatening to withhold love. Manipulators can also punish extraverts by making them miserable when socializing. A girlfriend, for instance, may flirt with other men when out on the town with her boyfriend.

Manipulators can also affect introverts by withholding affection. Since introverts prefer the company of only close friends, manipulators can force introverts to feel distressed by not allowing them to recharge their batteries alone. Many introverts require stimulation from cerebral exercises, so manipulators often force introverts to follow their whims by playing on an introvert's trustfulness.

Conscientiousness

People who are conscientious typically find comfort in attaining goals. If you are highly organized and ambitious, you possess conscientious personality traits. Studies have found the conscientious people are more likely to have empathy for others. Though agreeableness was the ultimate predictor of empathy, people who possessed both personality traits were concluded to have the greatest empathy.

Conscientious people are highly aware of others. They believe that a first impression lasts, so they take care of their appearances and are punctual. They believe they are obliged to act kindly to others, often afraid to offend. Non-conscientious people are more likely to behave spontaneously. They often have cluttered desks and do not care about punctuality. They are often blunt with others and state opinions easily. They find it easy to express opinions and are not afraid of disagreements. They are also less ambitious and do not find solace in success.

Conscientiousness changes with age. Studies have shown that older people are more likely to be conscientious than their younger counterparts. Children who have kinder parents are more likely to be conscientious as well. However, there may be a connection between biology and conscientiousness as well. MRI scans show there are variations in brain structure between conscientious and unconscientious people.

Highly conscientious people are excellent subjects for manipulators. Since they are easily convinced of offending someone, manipulators can use fear as a tool to control them. On the flip side, manipulators can also persuade conscientious people of their good attributes. In all, conscientious people are more suggestible than the other personality types.

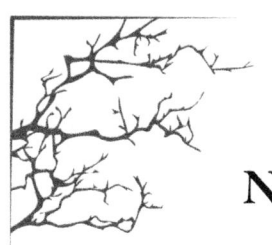

Neuroticism

Neuroticism is defined by the level of worry an individual experiences daily. Since there is a range of neuroticism from extreme worry about things beyond control and not a care in the world, it is not unusual to find wide varieties of reactions to stimuli. Neurotic people are highly volatile. They are more likely to experience jealousy and lash out against others due to small changes.

Neurotic people can react violently to change or perceived injustice. They are the people who fly into a fit of rage over rumors of infidelity or changes in status. For example, a highly neurotic man may throw dishes when his partner did not wash them. A woman may key a car if she finds her partner cheated on her. Though everyone experiences worry, emotionally unstable people cannot control their emotions.

On the other hand, people with greater emotional stability are able to adapt quickly to change. Emotionally stable people are often expressed as relaxed. Their worries, great or small, can be dealt with if they remain calm. They are more likely to maintain a healthy perspective. They are also more likely to be understanding of the faults of others, realizing that small problems are surmountable.

Early theorists believed there was a biological component to neurotic behavior. Hippocrates, the founder of modern medicine, believed that people with excess black bile in their stomachs behaved more irrationally. Modern science, however, has defined the behavioral inhibition system, which affects the way a person sees consequences. Neurotic people may overcompensate for their worries by acting in ways to prevent consequences.

Manipulators can easily manipulate neurotic people since they already constantly worry about consequences. Manipulators suggest negative consequences, and neurotic people act out, behaving irrationally. Emotionally stable people, on the other hand, require more cunning to persuade, often forcing manipulators to resort to manipulating their other personality traits.

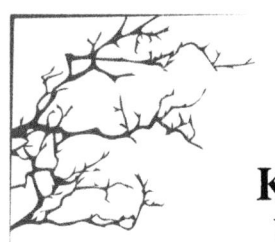

Know Your Neighbor

Everyone has a variation of the personalities listed above. However, to truly manipulate someone, you must know how to find their true desires. And, to do that, you need to get close to your target. The more someone knows you, the easier it is for you to manipulate them. That is why the vast majority of abuses and assaults happen from someone you know. They know how to either hide what they are doing to you or they manipulate you into believing that it is you at fault.

There are several ways to get to know the people around you. Being kind, doing favors for someone, or developing a personal relationship with someone are some of the best ways to do this. But, how do you develop trust? Some of the easiest ways to make someone open up to you is to listen.

Build Reliance

Think back to some of your most successful relationships. Likely, you were able to connect with someone and develop a sense of co-dependence: you were able to count on them, and they were able to count on you. A true manipulator knows how to make others believe they need someone for everything. When they believe you are trustworthy, manipulation begins.

Manipulators build up a target's self-esteem dependence. They make the victim believe they are perfect, effectively drawing them in. Targets often feel loved at first, like they found someone who will give them the self-esteem they need to go on in life. Since manipulators often victimize people who are vulnerable, manipulators make them believe they can be loved.

Listen and Talk

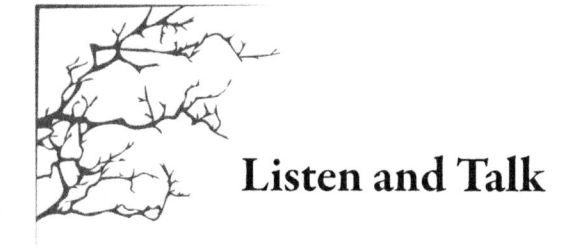

People are anxious to find someone who will talk with them about some of life's hardest problems. When life gets especially stressful, having someone to vent to aids in emotional and psychological health. People who are uncomfortable around others are often frustrated when their problems are unresolved and no one will listen to them. This creates a vicious cycle that forces many people to develop feelings of resentment toward society.

Allowing these people to open up is often difficult and frustrating, but it can be worth the effort. The best way to get started is to ask them direct questions. When you ask them questions like "What do you think of your mother?" they are often taken aback, but they are more likely to answer to direct questioning.

When you share with them your own vulnerabilities, they will start to trust more, seeing you as genuine. Psychologists agree that stating your vulnerabilities makes others feel safe. When they are ready to open up about their vulnerabilities, actively listen. Often, people who are closed have had troubles opening up in the past because others have made their opinions seem invalid. If you ask them about what they love, they will open up more, giving you insights into their true desires.

Validate their feelings and show them you care by using loving language. The phrase "But I shouldn't feel this way" is common for insecure people, proving they do not validate their own feelings. When you make them feel as though they have a right to feel the emotions they do, you immediately become a confidant. Love languages such as physical touch, gift giving, service, and words of affirmation cement your bond.

Use non-verbal communication to develop a sense of their feelings and attitudes. Signs such as folded arms, darting eyes, and fidgeting are all signs of discomfort. If you catch these signs, you can use different techniques to help them open up. If they have been hurt before, it may take several attempts to get them to confide in you.

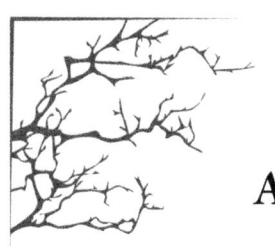

Acceptance

At the heart of nearly all human desire is the need for acceptance. Whether that is in the form of shared experiences or unconditional love, people need interaction to function properly. People who feel accepted are more susceptible to manipulation because they trust you.

Humans crave praise. When someone compliments you, endorphins in the brain make your body feel good. People who do not believe they are deserving of praise are far more vulnerable. To give them a taste of acceptance, compliments must be genuine and frequent. The more someone hears a compliment, the more likely they are to believe it, which may require the same input from many people.

Where do your eyes and attention go when someone interrupts a speaker? Do you immediately turn to the interrupter or to the original speaker? In many cases, people become closed because they believe others do not hear them, and paying attention to the original speaker or referring back to them may earn you high esteem. If you are the only person listening to them, you will become irreplaceable in their eyes.

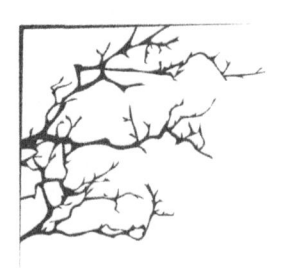

Practice

It may take time to understand all of the social cues associated with vulnerable behavior, but the only way to improve is to practice. If you often have a problem identifying non-verbal behavior, use film as a guide. Award-winning actors can make you believe their feelings with just a look.

Chapter 4: My Precious! Manipulation Through Emotional Response

Most people are ruled by their emotions or lack thereof. Someone who found out a spouse was cheating may feel disconnected and angry, choosing to lash out. A psychopath yearning to feel something may act violently by torturing and killing a victim for a twisted sense of pleasure.

Because the world is largely affected by emotions, humans are also easily manipulated through emotions. When you get close to someone else, they give you access to their emotions, providing a way for manipulation. Whether used for good or evil, manipulation of emotions is the most successful forms 0f persuasion in psychology.

Emotions for Exploitation

Pixar's *Inside Out* depicts a group of emotions running the brain of a child as she goes through difficulty adjusting to life after moving. The movie shows the most basic emotions: fear, disgust, sadness, anger, and joy. Though we are not run by small beings in our minds, the visual of these basic emotions shows how involved emotions are in daily life.

When it comes to manipulation, fear, anger, shame, and confusion are some of the easiest emotions to exploit. These emotions are easy to amplify and reduce, and continued manipulation on one person can make them like putty in your hands.

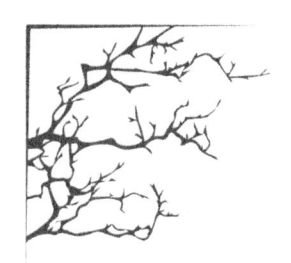

Fear

Fear is a basic human emotion that works into the biology of humankind. It is an instinctive emotion and is a necessary response for safety. Our first ancestors required the fight-or-flight response to keep them alive. Without it, they could easily have died from animal threats, starvation, or exposure. Fears common today come from these basic emotions instilled into our brains since the dawn of time. For example, many fear snakes and spiders because they posed a threat in the past. Venom from snake and spider bites could cause paralysis or death. Fear of the dark is common due to nocturnal threats when we lived in caves.

Children often still show signs of fear because they have not been conditioned to ignore basic instincts. Monsters in the closet are the results of the brain's attempt to identify sights and sounds. Since they have not had much experience with their senses, children's innate senses of fear try to keep them safe, even when there is no threat.

As time progresses, the need for fear becomes less important. We survive through visits to the grocery store, not through killing or growing our own food. We live in houses that provide safe havens from the world, and we have become soft due to regulated temperature.

However, fear is still an inherent part of the human experience, and manipulators use this emotion to sway individuals to masses. When the World Trade Center was hit on September 11, 2001, the media used fear as a way to control United States citizens. The phrase "If you see something, say something" became a tactic to encourage citizens to expose people of terrorism, despite many false cases. Because of the fear that something like this may happen again, people became more dedicated to their country.

In 2020, the fear of the Coronavirus kept many from leaving their homes. The media escalated the fear by encouraging people to panic, that this virus may wipe out millions or billions if not isolated, despite the efforts of doctors to calm the issue. The fear caused millions to stock up on toilet paper and hand sanitizer, encouraged by desperate attempts of others.

Fear draws blood from the brain to the extremities in the fight-or-flight mode, making it difficult to think. That is why many manipulators can keep their victims hooked for long periods of time. Fear can be addicting, which is why there is a holiday devoted to fear. Many associate fear positively due to distraction from other aspects of life. Manipulators mix the positive experiences of fear with the negative, addicting their victims to negative behavior.

Master manipulators use physical fear as a way to quell others into submission. For many, the threat of others physically overpowering them is enough to persuade them to do your will. However, if you do not have physical prowess, simple touch can also play a role in manipulating others. Invading personal spaces and direct eye contact make people uncomfortable and assert your dominance.

SUGGESTION: SECRETS OF COVERT MANIPULATION

Fear related to the withholding or uncertainty of love encourages easy manipulation. The unknown is a common fear, and persuading someone to believe that they will not receive love if they do not act according to expectations is a common tool. Manipulators use the roller coaster of loving emotions as a basis for fear.

Fear of becoming a social outcast persuades many to submit to peer pressure. Many use this as a subtle tool to prevent others from thinking properly. Mass hysteria and coddling of emotions often cause people to react fearfully.

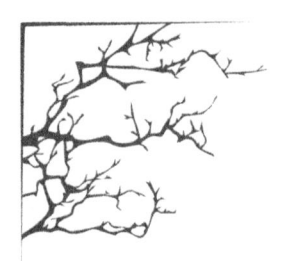

Anger

Anger is fear associated with blame. When a friend does not show up to a social event you created, you may feel anger due to your uncertainty of their friendship. When a partner does not express their love for you when you do for them, you may feel angry because you are afraid of losing love. If you encourage people to follow you on social media but they do not respond, you may feel anger because of your fear of becoming a social outcast.

When you get angry, your brain responds by killing neurons in the prefrontal cortex, effectively turning off a part of your decision-making skills. The hippocampus is also affected, killing neurons as well. This affects your short-term memory and prevents your brain from creating new neurons, which explains why it is difficult to remember what you are angry about.

Anger also causes a shortage of serotonin, the chemical that makes you feel happy. With this lacking supply, depression increases, and you are more likely to feel aggression. Constant anger lowers your immune system and bone density while increasing blood pressure and chances for headaches. If not controlled, anger can eventually lead to blood clotting and death.

Manipulators use anger to shock victims into submission. Often, manipulators cause anger in targets, forcing them to feel as though they are the reasons for the outbursts. However, once the situations escalate, manipulators use fear and blame their victims on their anger. Manipulators regulate their anger, often only appearing angry to cause submission. They then make note of the arguments, using their anger and the anger of their victims to punish them in the future.

Shame and Guilt

Shame and guilt are often confused with each other, but they are fundamentally different when viewing self-image. Feelings of guilt are associated with thoughts of "I did something bad," while shame asserts "I am bad." Shame asserts feelings of insecurity and unworthiness while guilt affects only actions.

Shame and guilt are some of the most damaging emotions, and they are surprisingly common. Students feel guilt when they forget to turn in an assignment, but professors can make students feel shame when they assert that the student did not turn in the assignment because they are stupid. A man can make his spouse feel guilty for flirting with another man, but his shame comes from believing that she has no value for causing the anger.

Shame and guilt were necessary in human evolution as they caused people to feel remorse and act with empathy. Living alone in early societies often proved a death sentence for people who were outcasts. The results of guilt are often positive, as they make humans kinder and more empathetic. It is designed to stop harm and encourage better behavior.

In the brain, shame and fear are very similar. They both shut off non-essential blood transfers to the brain, causing the body to experience fight-or-flight mode. Shame causes the brain to believe there is something wrong with it, making it difficult to feel relief. Shame strips away the power we feel to overcome difficult situations, lending to shame's vicious cycle.

Shame affects the way people see relationships. Children who are exposed to toxic shame when growing up do not know how true relationships should form and are often subjected to abusive relationships. Manipulators develop shame in their victims, making them believe that a toxic relationship is healthy. Victims of shame also often feel as though they deserve injustices because of some fabricated sense of insecurity.

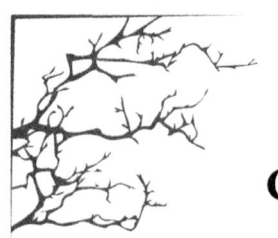

Confusion

Confusion is common in everyone, whether it is derived from the unknown, a lack of commitment, or a medical problem. Manipulators use confusion as a way to influence the way their victims think. If the target already has problems with commitment, a master manipulator may encourage them to believe their confusion is due to fear of the unknown. If the victim has a medical problem, a manipulator uses their confusion to make them believe the exploiter is the source of the victim's successes and joys, ultimately making the victim feel indebted to the manipulator.

Manipulators often use passive aggressive tactics to make their victims feel as though they are responsible for problems. Sarcasm, teasing, picking fights, and the silent treatment are just some ways for manipulators to encourage victims to do what they want. Manipulators make victims feel indebted to exploiters by claiming unwarranted successes.

Manipulators can also use confusion to offer clarity to those who suffer. If you want to help someone, you can manipulate others into believing in themselves. You can also provide them with senses of security by offering them your support when they are confused.

Techniques to Manipulate

The hard part is understanding how a person functions, but after that, manipulation only takes some practice with some very special techniques. The key to manipulation is identifying a person's vulnerabilities and then identifying which techniques are the most useful. Below are some of the most common techniques to use.

Love Flooding

Love flooding is showering someone with love, adoration, and attention, everything they would want when starting a relationship. Think of it as sending flowers, sending letters of love and devotion. It is chocolate and roses, smiles and spending time together. It is the most attention you have ever given anyone and ever will again.

It should come as no surprise that most people are susceptible to this at first. After all, who does not want to feel appreciated? However, this is how manipulators draw in their victims, developing a dependent relationship. After you shower them with gifts, tell them they owe you for everything you have done. You are the most important person in their lives because you give them everything they could ever want. Victims become trapped in a world of pleasure from which they cannot escape.

Narcissists use this method more than any others of the dark triad because they are used to doing it to themselves. They are good at giving compliments because they think the same of themselves. Narcissists love to give someone else attention because it makes them feel like they are the most important person in a victim's life. They can do anything they want as long as they continue to supply gifts and love letters.

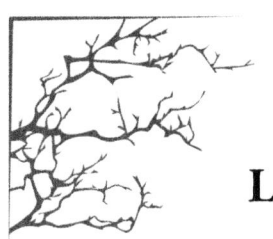

Love Denial

Love flooding is often accompanied by love denial, switching from black to white at the flick of a switch. Love denial is when love is withdrawn due to someone's actions or threats. Imagine when you were a kid and someone told you that you could not have the last cookie. Likely, you told them you hated them, not giving them any love in response to your disappointment. Children do this often because it is easy to manipulate parents into giving them love again.

Adults who do this to other adults or children likely experienced this behavior in their own childhoods. They believe that by withdrawing their love, their victims will be more likely to give in. However, this technique breaks down the bonds of love and often subjects both people to misery.

Manipulators who are not interested in the feelings of others might find that love denial is one of the best weapons in their arsenals. After all, their goal is to manipulate someone into believing they have to stay in a miserable relationship to remain happy. When you use this technique, start small and work up to smaller triggers for love denial. Use it as a punishment for their actions or threats. If they believe you will stop showering them with love and attention if they do not comply with your wishes, you can often make them do anything you want.

Fatigue Inducement

Fatigue breaks down the decision-making centers of your brain. Just think of the last time you spent an exhausting day at the office or have not been able to sleep for long periods of time. Physical and mental inhibitions form when fatigued. Studies show that your mental capacities lower by an average of 50% when you do not get a good night's sleep. For manipulators, this is the perfect time to pounce.

When someone is so trodden down that they can no longer fight back against manipulation, they are working on survival mode. They believe that fights are not worth the effort and that

SUGGESTION: SECRETS OF COVERT MANIPULATION

becoming a servant to someone's desires is better than the mental battery they receive every day.

Military officials often use fatigue inducement to persuade prisoners to give up secrets. Torture using fatigue inducement may involve asking the victim the same questions repeatedly while offering a punishment for wrong answers. Imagine fighting a spouse and calling them names on a daily basis. They may be independent enough to know you are trying to manipulate them, or they may simply crack under the pressure, starting to believe ill of themselves.

When manipulators get victims to this point, other manipulations are easier to perform. For example, if you mentally fatigue someone into believing they are worthless, love flooding will persuade them you are the only person who will ever love them. When you deny love, they will feel it is their fault, therefore absolving you of blame and mentally fatiguing them further.

Bribery and Gift-Giving

Bribery is one of the most common forms of child manipulation. Children will scream if they do not get what they want, thus forcing you to give them something to calm them down. However, this is not restricted to children. Adults use a reformed style of bribery to get what they want.

When a spouse behaves irrationally and badly, their partner may seek to offer a prize in return for happy behavior. Gold-diggers are some of the most common forms of manipulators using bribery. Beautiful men or women offer to spend time with rich people in exchange for gifts. A coworker may ask for a bribe to lean one way or another on an important issue. People who manipulate through bribery are often far more obvious than other types of manipulators due to evidence of services performed and gifts given.

Gift-givers expect something in return for their services or presents. Think of a salesman. They will often give away "discounts" to sell their products. They will also often offer small tokens when they want something. For example, a salesperson may award customers a "free" gift bag if they sign up for a makeup subscription for a year. A friend may offer snacks and presents but only if you come to their house to help them paint their fences.

Passive Aggressiveness

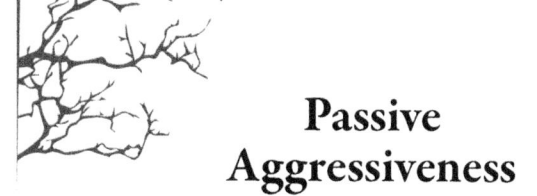

Some people make us feel uncomfortable, and it is hard to understand why. Much of the time, it is because a manipulator is using passive aggressive tactics to put you down without overtly stating so. A passive-aggressive phrase may subtly give themselves a compliment while putting you down. For instance, one woman may say to another, "I'm sorry that this dress is too small for you now, but it fits me perfectly." In this instance, the comment appeared to be concern but instead it insults.

Another form of passive aggressiveness comes in the form of sullen behavior. If you want to make someone feel badly, answer their innocent questions negatively. For example, if a woman asks a man, "What are you doing this evening?" a passive-aggressive response would be, "More than you are, by the looks of you." Though this example is more obvious, passive-aggressive responses are often tailored to insult others without their knowledge.

Stubbornness is a common manipulative tool to make others' lives miserable. Though stubbornness is not in and of itself exploitive, manipulatively stubborn people punish their victims through unwillingness to listen or act appropriately. Passive-aggressive people in a political argument may direct attention away from fact by stating their victim is a racist or sexist, refusing to admit that facts may support another's argument.

Passive-aggressive people take upon responsibilities and purposefully do not complete them. Of course, many people simply do not have the time or forget about obligations, but passive-aggressive people use lack of responsibility as a bargaining chip. For example, some grown children still exploit their parents by receiving a monthly allowance, even when they live alone.

Guilt Inducement

When someone states, "I need your help," they are opening themselves up to vulnerability, and true manipulators use the resulting empathy to persuade people to do things for them. When someone tells you they need help, many people are obligated to at least try.

Guilt inducement is different than asking for a favor. Manipulators often combine passive-aggressive behavior with guilt inducement. When someone denies help, manipulators behave sullenly, appearing to accept the denial but taking it badly. Manipulators make others feel shame for denying a request. Victims believe they are bad people at heart.

Dependency Inducement

Manipulators make others depend on them for comfort, survival, or help. Many people who get sucked into dependency are often people who feel a need for companionship. People who search online for an ideal partner are usually prime targets. They feel a need to be loved in order to feel worthy to live.

A common case of dependency inducement is the attachment of a partner living with a manipulator. At first, the manipulator showers them with gifts, but eventually starts doing whatever they want. The partner stuck in the relationship often begins to become financially dependent on the manipulator and believes they cannot leave because they would not be able to survive. Manipulators perpetuate this lie by making them feel guilty for purchases.

You can ensure dependency by first love flooding. Their sense of worth then comes from the gifts they receive. When the gifts stop, they believe they are the cause of discord, making them even more vulnerable.

Commitment and Consistency

Manipulators must be committed to their behaviors. If they fail to behave according to their patterns, victims have a chance to detect deception. That does not mean you cannot use a variety of these techniques to control your targets, only that you must be solely committed to your end goal.

The first step is to discover what it is you want to control. If you want your target to give you gifts, aim for a combination of guilt inducement and bribery. If you want your target to become a virtual slave to your whims, use a mixture of love flooding, love denial, and dependency inducement. Your goal should be to direct the thoughts of the people around you through charisma and affection, always with your end goal at the forefront of your mind.

Chapter 5: Words, a Weapon Not to Take Lightly

Actions are one thing, but words are some of the most important weapons in your arsenal. You can encourage people to love you, hate you, or admire from afar. There is a reason "the pen is mightier than the sword." You can create or destroy a reputation, and you can manipulate or influence others with just a phrase.

What do you think of when contemplating the word "manipulation"? It has a negative connotation suggesting that only

SUGGESTION: SECRETS OF COVERT MANIPULATION

unpleasant people use these tactics to affect the well-being of others. Now, what do you think of when contemplating the word "persuasion"? If you are like most people, you associate persuasion with a positive connotation. Persuaders are often depicted as people who use fact and positive ploys to get someone else to agree with them.

Persuasion and manipulation mean virtually the same thing, but you are more likely to convince someone of your opinion by claiming persuasion than manipulation. Words, therefore, are the cementing factors that will persuade someone to follow your lead or run the other direction.

Verbal Response Tactics

Verbal response tactics are far more than the words you use. They also involve voice inflections and changes in tones. If someone claimed they wanted to jump off a cliff in a joking matter, referring to an embarrassing moment, they would be seen in a far different light than someone with depressive tendencies. Just the pitch of your voice tells others your emotions.

Just like non-verbal techniques, verbal response tactics can manipulate others into believing or distrusting you. It all comes from how you speak and what you say. Master manipulators need practice with verbal responses to encourage people to follow them, watching others and improving their tactics for optimal results. Below are some common verbal response tactics that affect the success of your manipulation.

Confuse First, Suggest Second

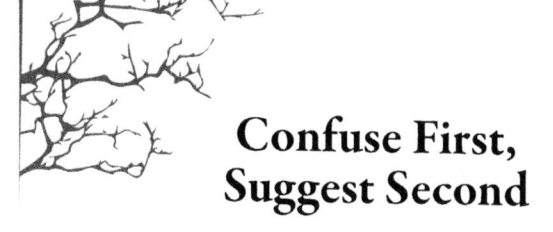

Confusion often has a bad connotation. For example, if you are confused about how to fix a problem, it often leads to frustration. However, many use confusion as a technique to separate the conscious mind from the unconscious. Hypnotists use these tactics to communicate with the unconscious mind by using gently confusing language, avoiding words that are overly informational or analytical. Instead, they speak in circles, but always make sense.

To illustrate, consider these words: "There is a part of you apart from the part that is part of understanding that takes part in the unleashing of your unconscious mind." Though the language given goes in a circle, if you read it through, it makes sense. The language is simply different from the language of which we are familiar. The goal is for the unconscious mind to understand while the conscious mind struggles to find out what you are talking about.

Your words must also contain some form of clarity, usually while your conscious mind is still working on your current phrase. After your confusing statement, issue a command. For hypnotists, their go-to command calls for sleep, but as a manipulator, you may issue a command for their trust. Since you are reaching the subconscious mind, you have greater access to their thoughts and desires, making them more suggestible.

When the brain is sufficiently confused and then receives a command, the subconscious will take over, ignoring the confusion and focusing only on the command. Your brain becomes so confused, so it looks for a way to escape. When you comply with the command, your mind can escape, leaving you in a hypnotic state.

Try, for example, to talk to someone for a long period of time using words that may add confusion. These words may include multiple meanings or simply be told in such a long string that they become confusing. At the end of your long speech, offer them a command. More often than not, their brains will reach for the command as a release and give you what you ask for.

Manipulators also like to catch you off guard. When you are not expecting a long conversation, your target's conscious mind starts to wander, leaving only the subconscious to listen intently. If you are reading this late at night or have been reading for a long period of time, you might find yourself in a trance-like state.

Here is another example. Follow the words as closely as you can as you continue to read the text or perform this test on someone else. *Place your right hand right on your left leg and your left hand right on your right leg. Let your left leg lie still as you notice your right hand right on the left leg. Feel your left hand leave your right leg and place it right over the right hand. Your left hand left on your right hand right in a warm spot left to lie on your right leg makes your chest feel warm as you imagine your arms securely at your side.*

SUGGESTION: SECRETS OF COVERT MANIPULATION

The combination of a long script and the various uses of right and left should have left your brain feeling confused. (Right?) The command at the end, therefore, offered your body an escape, and you will know if you were in a hypnotic state if your chest began to feel warm.

Most manipulators do not know about this trick explicitly. They have seen it work and have started to practice it on their own. For your own manipulation, practice is essential. Your speech must be relaxing and continuous, so know what you are going to say before you say it. Do not let yourself become confused as you practice this.

Alternate Manipulation

Alternate manipulation is the idea of putting thoughts into someone else's head and covertly asking them to act upon those suggestions. For example, if you wanted someone to get you an ice cream cone but it was rainy outside, you might say, "Do you feel like an ice cream cone? I'm really tired, but if you want one, then could you get me one, too?" In this case, you are not manipulating their emotions, only the way they think.

Another way to do this is to skirt around the issue, leading to a natural conclusion. Many businesspeople use this tactic to plant ideas into others' heads. If you are trying to get someone to stop wasting so much gasoline by going on many road trips, suggesting that they are using too much gas will probably only receive a nod from them, and they will not change anything. However, if you plant subtle messages in their mind regarding gasoline, you can change their opinions.

For example, instead of saying that gasoline is killing the environment and they are part of the problem, point out a news article that explains the country's dependence on foreign oil. Express your concern at the air quality of your city by pointing out black smoke coming from a large truck. If you try to persuade them with direct means, they will usually be-

SUGGESTION: SECRETS OF COVERT MANIPULATION

come defensive, but using more subversive techniques make them think that they reached a conclusion on their own.

Verbal Withdrawal

The silent treatment is often considered a highly immature type of manipulation, but it can work on a variety of levels, which makes it a narcissist's verbal weapon of choice. The silent treatment puts the manipulator in a position of control. They are responsible for the verbal communication, and no amount of begging will change their minds. In fact, they expect this reaction, preferring to force their victims to submit before they do.

The silent treatment also quells the arguments from the victim. Think of when you were a child and you implemented the silent treatment. You forced parents or siblings to come to you for an apology, disregarding their opinions entirely. The manipulator often appears as the one trying to keep the peace, preventing future arguing by remaining quiet. This often is accompanied by implied shame on the victim.

Narcissists often use this tactic when defending a bruised ego. Narcissists are highly insecure at their cores, so any ego bruising affects them profoundly. However, the silent treatment allows them to take control of their situations. When their victims attempt to communicate before the manipulator is ready or try to force an ultimatum, the manipulator may choose to end the relationship. Narcissists would rather be alone on their own terms than suffer the injustice of sacrificing their self-love for another.

The silent treatment is often most effective after you have already established a relationship with someone. This method is easily recognizable, and only people with mental fatigue or history of abuse may respond to it. Use your language as a source of positivity in your relationships. If you behave as a child during the silent treatment, you ultimately have less control of their actions.

Start by playing on their emotions when you want them to perceive hurt. Exploit their empathy by stating you have been in bad relationships before, and opening up has only hurt you in the past. Victims will start to see your silence as a trained response to previous hardship instead of manipulation. Commit yourself to the role of deception and follow the rules you have set for your silent treatment. For example, if someone refuses you friendship, become sullen and fearful, making your target expect that you had been burned by others in the past.

Choice Restrictions/ Limiting Options

When you limit the number of options you give others, they have little choice but to select one of your choices. For example, if your partner asks if you want to get some ice cream or a snow cone, you are expected to choose one of these options instead of choosing their own.

Salespeople frequently use this method of manipulation to create sales because customers are more likely to buy something if they are given only a limited number of options. For example, if a saleswoman were trying to sell a pair of jeans to a customer, she might suggest that either the customer select shorts or capri pants, displaying both of them. By saying that these two options are the best choices for the customer's figure, the saleswoman is more likely to make the sale.

Manipulators use choice restriction to persuade targets to believe only a handful of options. In many cases, these choices are black and white. For example, if a victim is having difficulty deciding whether or not to move in with their partner, the manipulator may give only two options: either you move in with me or we break up. Ultimatums force responses, which are usually in favor of the manipulator.

Manipulators also use more subtle ways to force a chosen response. They might, for instance, offer suggestions that would benefit both the victim and the manipulator but only respond favorably to one option. This form of manipulation occurs when manipulators try to encourage their targets to read their minds. Soon enough, manipulators do not need to evoke choice restriction as the victim has already discovered which will yield a positive response.

Leading Questions

Manipulators use leading questions to force victims to be consistent in their values. Leading questions are popular among charities and donation locations because they appeal to a target's sense of empathy, then prey on their commitments. For example, if a charity were to ask you if you care about saving trees and incorporating reforestation into logging companies, you would probably answer yes. After all, you would not want to appear as though you hate the environment. Once you have agreed to that, however, the charity then moves to more leading questions, such as "How much would you donate to help support reforestation?" You have already stated that you believe in the values of reforestation, so it is unethical to back out now. When they ask for money, you are caught in their trap.

When it comes to relationships, leading questions can force the victim of manipulation into believing they need to follow basic empathetic protocol and satisfy the manipulator. Questions such as "You want us to be closer, don't you?" make the victim feel obligated to the response that, yes, they do value closeness. Work relationships that value input from everyone in the company may be persuaded to choose a decision contrary to popular opinion due to leading questions.

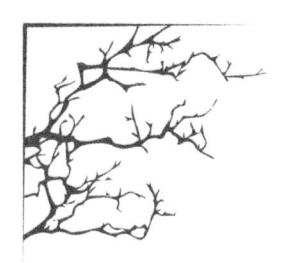

Sarcasm

Sarcasm is a thinly veiled attack on the intelligence and competence of others. Many believe that sarcasm is a sign of intelligence, and it does correlate with quick thinking, but sarcasm's true goal is to harm. It uses passive-aggressive language to make insults seem like a joke, and manipulators are masters of the art.

Sarcasm has a Greek root, which literally means to cut the flesh. Sarcasm is often a double-edged sword as well, since understanding and not understanding the nuances of the harmful joke can lead to ridicule. Sarcasm is a form of subtle bullying that lights up the pleasure centers of a manipulator's mind, making them feel quick-witted and clever.

However, their victims often feel small and belittled after sarcastic comments. They are subjected to shame, believing they are stupid. Manipulators terrorize their victims with fear of reprisal for given opinions, forcing the targets to close up within themselves. Sarcasm is often associated with emotional abuse due to its influence on a victim's brain, forcing fight-or-flight instincts to surface, sometimes causing physical problems.

An example for potential use of sarcasm may respond to a person's tendency to state the obvious. A manipulator would, in turn, respond, "No way. Way to go, Sherlock. You figured it out." For those who do not understand sarcasm, they may take the comment as a joke, however, ruining your intentions for manipulation.

Manipulators who seek to hurt others should be aware of the downside to constant sarcasm, however. When a victim becomes used to sarcasm, it becomes difficult to continue manipulating them this way. They often also develop a sense of sarcasm, giving as many insults as you produce. Many people become desensitized to sarcasm because of constant exposure. Just like with other forms of word play, sarcasm eventually becomes just another joke.

Lying and Exaggerating Truths

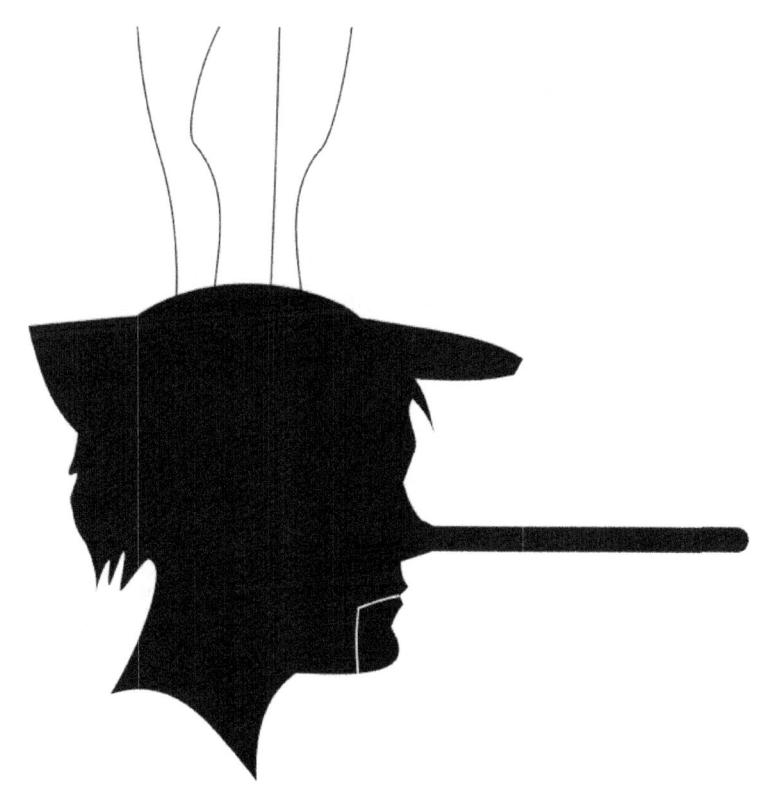

Lying is by far the most important tool in the manipulation endgame. After all, your manipulation is a form of lying. Lying keeps you one step ahead of your target. You are in control of your situation when you can lie about what is happening in your relationships.

Most manipulators lie to themselves, to their peers, to everyone. This is often in direct response to the dark triad. People who exhibit qualities associated with narcissism, Machiavellianism, and psychopathy do not feel emotions readily, so lying is a way to feel emotion and convince others of your sincerity.

People who are burdened with excessive feelings of empathy can only lie due to extensive practice. Liars need control of their voice inflections and non-verbal cues that tip victims off about manipulation. Experienced liars have spent many hundreds of hours perfecting their body language to effectively lie. Anyone can learn to do it if they spend enough time regulating breathing and standing in front of a mirror.

Experts who look for liars usually try to look for a list of behaviors and patterns that affect the liar's life. However, only over half of people can tell if someone is lying. Considering the chances for guessing if they are lying is 50%, these are not very convincing odds. People rely on their gut instincts to tell them if they are being lied to, which frequently involves unconscious detection. Therefore, to avoid detection, practice these methods of detection in the mirror and with friends to perfect your lying.

1. *Body Language*

The hands are the first places most detectives look to determine lying because they are often extremely expressive. For example, when someone is lying, they tend to make hand gestures after finishing the story as opposed to before or during the conversation. This is because liars have already rehearsed their lies often, making their lies a matter of fact instead of an emotional response.

Liars are also more likely to gesture with both hands. Studies have shown that people who lie use both hands 15% more than those who do not (Jalili, 2019). Liars also face their palms inward when speaking. The unconscious mind demonstrates that it is holding something back and displays it outwardly. In many cases, they hide them altogether, putting their hands in their pockets or under a table.

Liars also fidget. When under stress, the central nervous system causes the body to experience itching and restlessness. Liars who are unused to lying are more prone to these behaviors because they are more difficult to control. Practice hiding your restlessness when nervous by stopping your leg from hopping or scratching your face.

1. *Facial Expressions*

The true master manipulator is also one of the best poker players because they hide their emotions in their faces well. When you begin to lie, study master actors to see how their facial expressions change with stimuli. Liars must be able to both cloak their true feelings and express expected emotions. For example, if you are privy to knowing about a surprise party your friends are throwing for you, you must appear surprised when you get there, even though you are not.

Your eyes must also be masked when lying. Though there is no definitive proof that the ways that eyes point show if they are lying or not, many theories conclude that skirting eyes are common in liars looking for a response, especially if they are caught off guard. However, another study concluded that liars are more likely to stare into their victim's eyes longer than those telling the truth. To be safe, observe eye movement in others to determine your own way of bending the truth.

Pursing the lips or hiding them from view is another sign of guilt. People who are under investigation often curl their lips back when they are lying by omission, and a tight mouth is generally a sign of guilt.

Liars must also watch their complexion. Liars often experience changes in blood flow to the face, causing it to either go white or turn bright red. This is caused by a fear response. Liars are also more prone to sweating or dryness, the latter frequently affecting the mouth. The only way to combat this is to practice. If you practice breathing easily, you can more effectively control your heart rate and blood flow.

1. *Tone and Content of Speech*

Nervousness affects the way people speak. If you are unconvinced, attend a lecture from someone who does not often speak publicly, then talk with them afterward. The pitch of their voice may change dramatically when in front of others. They may also increase their volume. Biologically, vocal cords tighten when nervous, causing a rise in voice tonation. Combat this through breathing exercises and slight pauses.

Liars who try to convince others of their sincerity usually go overboard. They start to use words like "honestly" or "truthfully," almost as if they are trying to convince themselves of the lie. Studies have also shown that people who use more filler words—such as "um," "uh," or "you know"—are more likely lying. That is because they are trying to fill the time to come to another conclusion, forcing their minds into overdrive.

If you are new to lying, be aware of what you are saying at all times. Uncomfortable liars are more likely to slip up than those who have practiced their stories extensively. Crime shows are not far off when depicting people who slip up or change their stories. It is very common, so practice what you say.

1. *Backward and Forward*

Liars are often so focused on keeping their verbal and non-verbal tells from detectives that they forget the essence of the lie: the story. Many lie detectors can tell if someone is lying based on how they tell a story in reverse. Liars have rehearsed their stories so many times in their heads that it is easy to tell it in chronological order, but when they start to reverse the process, they often reveal cracks in their stories.

Liars must become so well versed in their own lies that telling a lie becomes a truth in their own minds. Just as truth-tellers have to stop to analyze their stories or change the inflections of their voices, so must liars learn how to mimic normal speech. Psychopaths are exceptionally good at this step as they convince themselves as well as they convince others that they are sane.

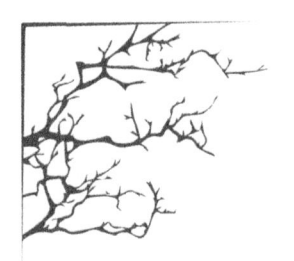

Reward

Reward your targets verbally and non-verbally for your manipulation. For example, if you plant the idea to give up eating unhealthy foods in your target's head, when they finally give in to the behavior, reward them for thinking it on their own. They will become accustomed to your praise when they start to think like you do.

If you have manipulated correctly, your victims should be able to at least partially read your mind. Many manipulators have simple end goals, like helping someone overcome grief or trapping someone in a committed relationship; therefore, interpreting their true desires is easy. When you continue to reward positive reactions to your manipulations, they will see you as a source of positive energy and will aim to please you.

Chapter 6: The Magic of Reverse Psychology and Talking Around an Idea

People respond to commands in various ways, but it is unlikely you will find people willing to do whatever you say whenever you say it. Many people naturally fight against what others tell them to do by doing the exact opposite. Think back to when you were a child and your parents wanted you to clean your room. If you were a rebellious child, chances are you went out with your friends or lay in your room and pouted.

However, when you see this behavior as a parent, you can change the way your child responds by becoming aware of what your child is thinking. You might, instead, try to get them to clean their room by stating you love it dirty when they are angry with you. Of course, this juvenile reaction to commands only lasts so long in children, but there are other ways to use it into adulthood.

Reverse Psychology Introduction

We all use reverse psychology in some way. If you have ever wanted something so badly that you actually convinced yourself that you do not want it, you used reverse psychology. In some cases, imagining the worst can make you feel better, and many use this as an escape from difficult situations.

Using reverse psychology is often a gentler form of manipulation because it encourages others to come to their own conclusions. Of course, the conclusions you are giving them are very limited options, but if you are smart about it, they will not notice. For example, if you want a new ring but you do

SUGGESTION: SECRETS OF COVERT MANIPULATION

not want to buy it yourself, you can tell your partner about it, specifically tailoring your words into explaining that you do not want it. If they are naturally compelled to buy you gifts, they will likely take the bait.

You must understand your logical conclusions to coerce someone into doing the opposite of what you suggest. When a boulder is set in motion down a hill, it does not stop, and the same logic applies to people. If you first set your ideas in motion, they will snowball, leaving you to do little by standing back and watching the person you are manipulating do your bidding.

Reverse psychology is often disputed because it can have negative effects on relationships. If used too often, a victim will feel as though they are being constantly manipulated, effectively ending relationships. If you are looking for a way to fix your own or others' relationships, contact a psychological professional.

Compliant vs. Resistant People

Have you ever noticed when manipulating others that some are easier to coerce than others? Some people trust and share vulnerabilities easier than others, while their resistant counterparts often feel obligated to keep up walls. In many cases, this may be because of personality traits, but some people have developed resistant traits from past experiences.

Since reverse psychology is more obvious than other methods, it will not work on everyone. Compliant people are more likely to go with the flow, while resistant people find obeying someone's order degrading. For most cases, resistant people are easier to manipulate with reverse psychology, so it is important to identify key characteristics before you begin.

Emotional and overbearing people are primary targets for reverse psychology. Just like the child who refused to do what they were asked because it was not what the parent wanted, emotionally volatile people are more likely to respond, especially when irritated.

How to Do It

Do not think of a pink elephant. If you thought of a pink elephant, you are not alone. Most people, when told not to do something, do the opposite. The concept of what I will call the "don't look" principle draws others' attention away from distractions to a point of focus.

1. Present an Option

Intonation is very important. Using calm speech sets others at ease and prevents them from recognizing your manipulative intent. Adults are more mature than children, making subtlety essential. Speak to your target in a friendly, confident tone, perhaps adding a flippant air to your words. When you appear to not care if your suggestions are adhered to or not, people are more set at ease.

Consider, for example, someone who pleads to be a part of a group. Instead of using likeable or agreeable personality traits, they rely on the mercy of others to get what they want. Now, consider someone who acts forthcoming and friendly, using charisma to gain a position in the group. The cooler actions make the agreeable person seem like the better choice.

If you use a pleading tone when presenting options for reverse psychology, both compliant and resistant people will likely shut down the attempt at reverse psychology. However, when you appear to not care about the results, both resistant and compliant people will be more interested in entertaining your thoughts.

Using reverse psychology requires you to make the first step, implanting an idea in your target's mind. If you want to go to a movie but the rest of your immediate friends want to go clubbing, make an excuse to bring up a movie, then second guess yourself. If your friends have empathy for you, they will become interested in your suggestion. If they are not, it may require more manipulation to make them comply.

1. *Make It Enticing*

If your friends have no interest in going to the movie, make it sound like the more enticing option. For example, if your friends love popcorn at the movie theater, suggest that you could get an extra large bag. If your friends have trouble sitting through a movie, suggest seeing a terrible comedy or B-movie, encouraging them to remember when they laughed at both the movie and yourselves for going to see it.

If it has been some time since you have seen a movie, plan ahead, showing your friends a movie you all love. Select an option that is in the same genre as the movie you want to see, encouraging them to think about the fun they had recently. Continue to drop hints about what makes seeing the movie so important to you while watching it without outrightly expressing your desire to go to the movies.

1. *Use Non-Verbal Cues*

SUGGESTION: SECRETS OF COVERT MANIPULATION

Some of the more obvious non-verbal cues, such as sighing when watching a movie, establish your desire to go out. You can also resort to more drastic measures, such as playing a movie on your phone when you go clubbing with your friends. True friends will see that you are not enjoying yourself and will feel indebted to you. You can use this as leverage to express your love for seeing movies while spending time with them.

Simple touches of the arm or eye contact also make people more susceptible to manipulation. Therefore, when you talk about wanting to go to the movies, touch them on the shoulder or arm and smile. This form of manipulation will force them to associate positive energy with your touch and presence. Touch has been proven to persuade people, so use it to your advantage.

1. *Discourage or Argue*

The mark of a true reverse psychology ploy is discouragement. Make it appear as though you want something but do not want to bother others by forcing your opinions on them. When you argue with your own point, obstinate people are more likely convinced that you need what you are manipulating for.

When your friends suggest going to the movies, reply, "We don't have to. It is out of the way and I'm the only one who wants to go." Your friends will likely be manipulated into believing that you regard your own opinions as lesser than the group. They seek to lift you up by giving you what you want.

Friends who want to argue with your choices may strongly advocate for going to a movie if you show interest in clubbing. You may use the opportunity at the club to become an embarrassment to your friends, revealing too much or talking too loudly and rudely. When friends see that you will behave irrationally when going to a club, they will often vehemently argue with you when you suggest going back, giving you leverage.

1. *Push Them to Make a Decision*

Make your target believe that they are in charge of the decision. When they feel in control, they become easier to manipulate. A friend may argue, "I'll decide" when you express your desire to do something contrary to your goal. Make them think you are giving them the control by using language such as, "Ultimately, it is your decision."

Your friends will conclusively think that it was their decision to go see a movie. The subliminal marketing you did for your agenda made your option not only viable, but preferred.

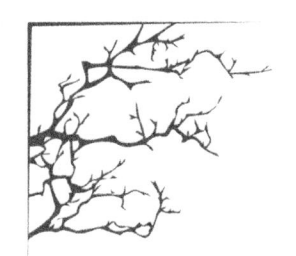

Context

Though the rules for reverse psychology are straight-forward enough, it also requires doing the preceding steps at the right place and the right time. Before you can convince someone to do anything, you have to ignite their curiosity. The brain releases dopamine when curiosity is aroused, stimulating the brain. So, when you ignite someone's curiosity through manipulation, they actually enjoy the experience.

Developing a deep connection with your target often creates a greater sense of curiosity in the victim. Think about if a stranger told you that you would make a fine member of their crew setting out to sea. Though it might pique your interest, you would likely find it more creepy than anything else. However, if someone you know suggested that you join them on an ocean adventure, the pleasure centers in your brain would light up.

Of course, all of this depends on the timing. For example, if you were to suggest to a friend to go shopping during a funeral, even using reverse psychology, you would not receive a great response. However, after the funeral is over, you may subconsciously suggest to your friend that retail therapy may be beneficial to help you get over your grief. The difference of even a few hours plays a large role in the effectiveness of reverse psychology.

Personality type also plays a significant role in the effectiveness of reverse psychology. When targeting someone with a closed mind, they will likely see through your act immediately. However, if you get them to open up, you have a greater chance at success. People who are highly neurotic may be some of the best subjects for reverse psychology since they are already highly susceptible to changes in emotion.

Remember also that humor is reverse psychology's greatest ally. Delving too deeply into manipulative tendencies when using reverse psychology often makes it obvious. Instead, create a light-hearted atmosphere that makes people who are subject to your manipulation eager to spend more time with you.

Have fun with reverse psychology. There is a reason there are so many cartoons associated with it. You may also experience success with extreme uses of reverse psychology. When you use statements like, "There is no way I would ever want to

SUGGESTION: SECRETS OF COVERT MANIPULATION

do this thing that I have always wanted to do with you," manipulators may make targets laugh, making your apparent disregard to subtlety the standard for reverse psychology in the future.

Reverse psychology can also help you become closer to your target when you consider what they need. When considering another, you can more effectively predict what they will or will not do for you. Tailor your manipulation to how your target reacts to your manipulation. Use more subtle reverse psychology for emotionally unstable people and try to exaggerate it for more open people.

Always, remember what your end goal is. The best strategies have a plan, and they could last for years, gently coercing someone to marry you or be as short as making someone fetch you a sucker. The larger your favor, the bigger your plan should be. Manipulators always use their ultimate goals to continue their motivation for manipulation.

Finally, be aware of the person you are trying to coerce. Though reverse psychology may simply not work, many times it also results in much worse consequences, such as broken friendships or mistrust. Use your discretion and only use reverse psychology when you are either sure it will work or have no regard to maintaining relationships.

Chapter 7: Your Subconscious Mind: Use of Subliminal Influence

When most people think of subliminal influence and messaging, they think of futuristic attempts to control the public's mind. The flashing of screens could put people into hypnotic states, forcing their subconscious to believe they need whatever product the advertisers say they do. However, subliminal messaging is used today in the form of vocal and imagery placement.

What Is a Subliminal Message?

There is nothing futuristic about subliminal influence. You are simply influenced by your previous experiences, whatever they may be. For example, you may feel anxious when you hear disco music if your mother left you in the car when she grocery shopped in the 1970s. You may feel the need to dance when you see an iTunes advertisement if, every time you saw one when you were a kid, you struck the pose.

Subliminal messaging has been around for thousands of years, mostly because the practice continues to work. Ancient Greeks first thought of the idea to influence people using words. They believed putting an idea in someone's head would help them develop an unconscious need for it.

Ivan Pavlov, a psychologist investigating conditioning responses started an experiment with dogs. Whenever Pavlov would ring a bell, he would feed the dogs. Soon, when the bell would ring, the dogs would start to salivate, proving that responses can be conditioned. *The Office* (U.S.) used a similar joke on its television show, displaying Dwight's conditioned response of taking an altoid after every time Jim shut down his computer.

Subliminal messaging really gained grounds in the 1900s though when advertisements became popular. Science began to unlock the influence of subliminal messaging and turned it into an art. Various bogus scientific attempts tried to prove that flashing a word across a television screen would encourage viewers to buy whatever was suggested. However, studies in the 21st century did prove that subliminal messaging had a way of affecting people if they were already considering that option.

For example, creators of *The Simpsons* tried to induce people to buy products related to thirst, which should be obvious if you are aware of Homer Simpson's drinking track record. If *The Simpsons* showed an episode that displayed high levels of thirst, viewers were more likely to buy products presented on the screen.

Action Priming

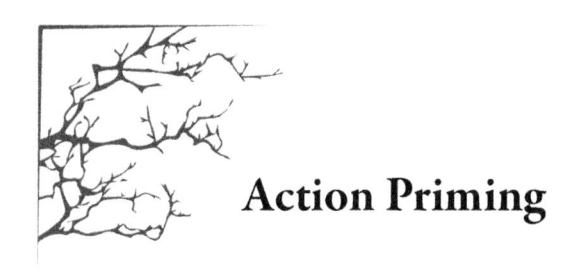

Today, subliminal messaging comes from parents, media, and other close influencers. For example, if every time you saw an ad for cigarettes your mother or father told you that you would get cancer, the word "cancer" became synonymous with pictures of black lungs and the throat-closing conclusion that you may get cancer from smoking. This is also referred to as subliminal priming.

Subliminal priming is below the surface. Every repeated action in your life has some connection to subliminal priming. Girls who grow up with the intentions of marrying a prince have probably spent a lot of time watching *The Little Mermaid* and *Cinderella*. Below the beautiful fairytale stories, some children are conditioned to believe that they must simply lose a shoe to meet royalty.

No one has told these girls that they have the potential of meeting a prince, as the likelihood of marrying one is less than one in a million. However, when conditioning began, they did not consciously notice what they were being taught. They were convinced of their royal potentials because they failed to attach logic to subliminal messaging, which is common in children.

However, subliminal messaging is often weak if not constantly reinforced. When factors such as the environment or relationship statuses change, people become aware of their subconscious desires. Though the messages themselves may be only seconds long, the longer the amount of time our minds are subjected to the messaging, the more likely we are to respond in the future.

Absolute Threshold

Subliminal messaging targets the absolute threshold of the unconscious mind. An absolute threshold refers to the smallest amount of stimulus the mind can comprehend. Of course, people respond to it only about half the time, so marketing ploys require extended usage to make an impact.

The absolute threshold for hearing is the lowest tone the ears can hear without interference. The ticking of a clock in the background may be the lowest sound heard in the room, so your subconscious will become hyper aware of the noise. Children are more subjected to lower and higher tones because the absolute threshold for noise becomes more limited with age. This is perhaps why children are more susceptible to subliminal persuasion than adults.

The absolute threshold for hearing corresponds to the smallest amount of light you can see. The best way to determine this for yourself is to light a candle in a dark room. The further away you get from the candle, the dimmer it becomes. Your absolute threshold refers to the furthest away you can see the light half of the time. Marketers use visual absolute thresholds when designing products. For example, Coca-Cola's brand is highly protected because of the way that it makes their customers feel. The font and the colors make the brand stand out.

Smell's absolute threshold can be relatively small compared to the other senses. After all, some senses are far more potent for others. For example, the gas pumped has a very distinctive smell. The gas itself is odorless, but they put in the smell to alert people if there is a gas leak. Even a small amount of a gas smell is enough to get you calling an electrician. Bakeries use smell to encourage customers to get products. The absolute threshold for smelling cupcakes is small, so they use other, stronger smells to draw you in, even if you are not in sight of the bakery.

The absolute threshold for touch is the lightest an object can touch your body that you can feel. The hands and lips are some of the most sensitive places for touch, so experiment with your own absolute threshold to determine how little it takes for marketers to affect you. When you touch something, you are more prone to buy it, like that shiny red car you saw at the dealership. Manipulators encourage touch by making surfaces with a variety of textures.

Taste is the last sense that manipulators use to sway opinions. The absolute threshold is the smallest amount of taste you can sense. Obviously, restaurants and grocery stores want you to become hooked on the taste of their products, so many goods are enhanced to keep you coming back. Taste is the most difficult form of manipulation because of common sense and general laws: you should not lick the sidewalk, neither is munching on chips as you walk through the store looked upon favorably. However, taste brings back memories. People who find comfort in sweet foods may have had them as a child. Memories, in the end, are some of the most important marketing tools.

Subliminal Influence

It has been established that there are many ways that subliminal messages influence the way we perceive the world. But, how do you create your own subliminal influences to affect the people you want to manipulate? You must first give people the illusion that they are selecting on their own. Targets must want what you want.

Priming refers to changing the way a person's brain responds to stimulus. The senses listed above can change or amplify feelings associated with them. For example, the Pixar movie *Ratatouille* takes advantage of subliminal priming. In Ego's youth, he was presented with the dish ratatouille to make him feel better. The taste brought him to his past, making the simple dish extraordinary in his eyes.

When manipulating others, especially for the long haul, implementing priming techniques can make future manipulations easier. You can make your targets feel happiness by explaining that they are a good person, or you can destroy their self-esteem by showing them a picture of themselves you have shamed in the past.

Priming is how manipulators keep people coming back again and again. Though exploiters ultimately affect the way people feel by associating an object or word with a positive or negative response, they are able to escape blame by insisting their targets' responses are associated with something else.

Semantic Priming

Semantic priming refers to the priming of language. Word association brings out what most people perceive when using semantic priming. For example, saying the word "dog" is often associated with the word "cat." If the assumption is made toward a dog and a wolf is introduced, semantic priming has taken effect. The way the brain associates language is through logic or visual connections, such as bananas and the color yellow.

You may semantically prime someone by associating a behavior with the words "good" or "bad." Parents use this tactic often to teach their children how to behave. When the children throw a tantrum, parents label the outburst as "bad" and perhaps institute a punishment. However, this type of semantic priming can backfire as, later in life, the children do not know how to accurately portray their feelings, often letting them fester, resulting in shame for future outbursts.

Visual Priming

Visual priming changes the way people think about images. One of the most common forms of this lies in cartoons. Bugs Bunny was known for changing the way we see rabbit season. His presence in the cartoon "What's Opera Doc?" influenced the way many children viewed Wagner's "Ride of the Valkyries." Many children who grew up with this cartoon now associate this famous opera with a cross-dressing bunny.

Visual priming has proven to last longer than semantic priming because it is associated with sight. Though there are many uses for words, visuals do not change readily. Increased exposure to the visuals often further cements the subliminal message. Marketers use this strategy to get people to identify everyday objects with the visual priming. One example of this is television's use of colors. Logos that use a wide array of colors, like NBC's logo, make people feel happy. The bright colors create a flow of pleasurable chemicals in the brain, making you think that NBC will offer exciting programming.

Studies have shown that repetition affects the brain's ability to process visual images. When tested with a group of adults, images were flashed in front of their eyes in random order, each image repeating 10 times. Even though their exposure to the images were brief, the subjects could accurately identify each of the images.

The next study used images that were familiar with everyone, like photos of animals or landscapes. They then subjected the participants to the images again, this time only repeating some of the images. The images that were repeated were more recognizable, even though the images that were not repeated were in view longer.

When images flash quickly in front of you, it takes an additional second to recognize what you saw. For example, imagine an image with a tree and an owl, everything in almost the same colors. When you look away (or think of something else), immediately try to identify what you saw in the image. Do not go back to look at it until you have come to a conclusion.

If you are like most people, it probably took you a few seconds to realize that there was an owl in the tree. However, when you condition your brain to see the owl, you cannot "unsee" it. The more you go over the image, no matter the length of time, the more obvious it is that the owl is present.

SUGGESTION: SECRETS OF COVERT MANIPULATION

Some visual priming also leads to suppression. If you have seen the same face in social media and can put a name to it, studies have shown that your brain is less likely to need repetition. Unlike the image above, a photograph of Kim Kardashian is more likely to be recognized because names do matter. So, to manipulate through visual priming, put a name to the face of the visual.

Positive and Negative Priming

Positive and negative priming refer to the processing speed in which you ingest information. For example, using the color example in Chapter 2, remember that the color of the words was different than the words themselves. It was more difficult for your mind to process the color of the ink because you are conditioned to react first to the words. Reading the words is an example of positive priming, since the process was quick, regardless of the color of the ink.

However, if you had to focus only one letter at a time to read the colors faster, you experienced negative priming. Your mind shuts out the rest of the information on the page to help your processing speed. You read the colors at a slower rate, but you were still able to do so accurately.

Negative priming forces the brain to differentiate between two types of responses. Imagine a picture that is a combination of two images. Though your brain eventually recognizes that the image shows a product in the window and a person's reflection overlapped, it likely took you a second to accurately decipher the image. This is called inhibition negative priming.

SUGGESTION: SECRETS OF COVERT MANIPULATION   149

The episodic negative priming theory suggests that when you remember an image with multiple stimuli, you only retrieve one part of it at a time. For example, if you were to remember the image above, you may only remember the telephone pictured. However, you may next remember the reflection of the man. In either case, your memory is likely flawed since you are only remembering part of the image.

To influence people using negative and positive priming, get them to notice simple parts of your speech or images you show them. Since people are better able to process black and white versions of stories and visuals, you will experience more success when associating positive responses with positive priming. If you want to hide a part of an argument that was your fault or want to encourage your victim to think that it was their fault for a negative response, use negative priming to redirect their focus.

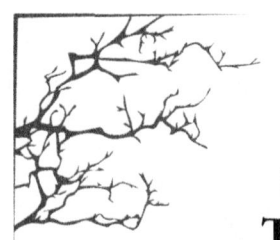

Using the Techniques

Priming is the art of familiarity, which means you may need to redirect your target's focus back to your stimulus multiple times. Start by introducing your manipulation in passing. For example, if associating the word "bare" with words that induce feelings of shame, first use language that makes them focus on the word. You might say, "That bare woman is awful for showing her body." The image of a bare woman now dissuades the target from feeling sympathy or arousal.

As soon as you introduce priming, slip it into everyday conversation. Use examples that support your theories. If you want your partner to stop liking dogs, associate their visuals with dirt and grime. Insinuate that you want to keep a clean house and dogs would only mess it up. When walking in the park, point out a dog's negative reaction to another dog, forcing your partner to view dogs through a tainted lens. Enforce the theory that dogs would only add a burden to your life by making your partner see the relationship only in black and white.

Once you have enforced your manipulation, continue to hint toward your reasons for your decision. Make them believe your manipulation was their idea, that the suggestions you planted are what will make them happy. Remember, stay calm

SUGGESTION: SECRETS OF COVERT MANIPULATION

and do not rush into anything. If you sound too rushed, they will recognize what you are doing.

Other Ways for Delivering a Subliminal Message

Delivering a subliminal message is often time consuming, but ultimately highly effective. But what if you do not have the time to spend hours revising ways to send a message to your target through persuasion? There are other methods to give you the same results as priming your victims but do not last as long. If you are looking for a quick way to make someone consider your agenda, try one of these options.

The Benjamin Franklin Effect

The Benjamin Franklin effect comes from its name: Benjamin Franklin. When conversing with a rival, Benjamin Franklin asked to borrow a book. When his rival conceded to the request, Franklin sent him a letter stating how much he enjoyed it. They became friends afterward, simply because of this request.

It may seem logically contrary to assume that asking a favor would result in a change of heart, but the idea goes deeper than that. The mind is not comfortable with dissonance, so it tries to justify its actions. In the case above, Franklin's rival wanted to lend him the book, but his feelings of dislike affected his decision. Ultimately, his rival resolved the dissonance by concluding that he liked Franklin better than he thought.

This method is commonly used today. When an unliked coworker asks for help in a difficult project, you may feel the desire to help them. In response, you feel your own dislike start to fade. Your coworker showed their vulnerabilities, which prompted you to feel merciful.

As long as your target feels you are worthy of receiving help, their brains will provide justification for granting you a favor. However, putting someone on the spot during requests can have a backfiring effect. The person who is obligated to grant you a favor may now resent you for making them feel embarrassed if they do not respond favorably.

Another theory states that when others grant favors for people they do not like, they receive a personal reward: higher esteem and a good feeling. People perform service to not only make others feel good but to give themselves a temporary high. They may pattern their behaviors after others and conclude that granting favors will make them seem like a better person to their peers. After a favor is granted, the target often feels respected by the manipulator, encouraging them to help time and again.

Big Favor, Small Favor

Do you remember a time when a friend or family member asked you for a huge favor, like house sitting for a few days while they were away? If they knew you had a very busy schedule and would find it difficult to do what they wanted, they might ask for a smaller favor, to which you might have felt obligated to perform, like feeding their cat occasionally.

This form of manipulation, self-named the Big Favor, Small Favor principle, preys on others' empathy. After all, you have already disappointed them once, so you do not want to do it again. The target may even feel relieved that you will be satisfied with the second request. Studies have shown that asking an outlandish request first is the key to getting your target to grant your favor. If you start with your lower deal, they will likely decline, so always start off large.

The Big Favor, Small Favor principle is also used in marketing and sales ploys. Think of the last time you went to buy a car. Likely, you tried to talk the salesperson down from their set price, so a negotiation ensues. The salesperson insists that they will be losing money if they do not sell it for the list price, and you will be missing out on a great deal. However, when the two of you come to an agreement, you feel satisfied with what you accomplished.

On the salesperson's side, however, they have pulled the wool over your eyes. Many dealerships price the cars at prices that are far higher than they expect to get for the cars. A car's cost to the dealer including overhead may cost $15,000, but they could mark it as $25,000, anticipating to lower the price slightly. If the customer is not a good negotiator, the salesperson may make the sale with an additional $10,000 dollars. But, if the customer does talk them down a couple thousand dollars, they will still see a high profit margin.

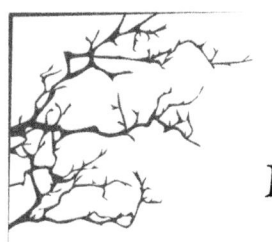

Mirroring

Some people are naturally adept at mirroring others. Children with heroes often mimic the way they save the day. Adults who respect and idolize people in the workplace often try to think as their heroes would and perform similar tasks. There is a reason mimicry is considered the sincerest form of flattery.

Though many people mirror subconsciously, you can practice mirroring consciously as well. Point out your target's good qualities and show them your emulation. They may try to take you under their wing. People are flattered when they realize others' respect for them. Praise is one of the most craved desires of the human race, so others showing their support of you through copying your actions gives your brain an extra dose of endorphins.

However, mirroring can also be an incredible disadvantage if you do it too frequently or with too much vigor. No one likes a "yes man," so simply agreeing with everything your target says may put them off. If someone followed you everywhere and was in awe of everything you did, you may feel a creepy vibe.

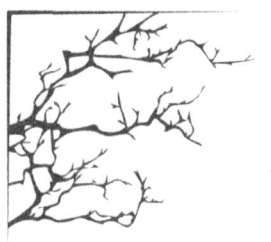

Tiredness

When was the last time you agreed to someone just so you could go home and sleep? People who are tired do not want to put up a fight, which makes them highly susceptible to subliminal messaging. For example, if you want to go to the zoo with your partner in the morning, mentioning it several times as they are getting ready for bed may encourage them to say yes, just to shut you up.

Children unconsciously use this method frequently. Since parenthood is naturally draining, asking parents for a favor after a long day will most likely get a positive response. Even small actions like mentioning the need for a new breakfast cereal when a parent or partner is tired is often enough to promise you the new cereal in the morning.

When tired enough, the body runs on autopilot. That means your feet act while your brain sleeps. Your subconscious is keeping your body active while tired. So, talking to a tired person gives you direct access to their subconscious. You can use hypnotic techniques to further encourage the subconscious to surface, giving you access to your target's desires and easy manipulation.

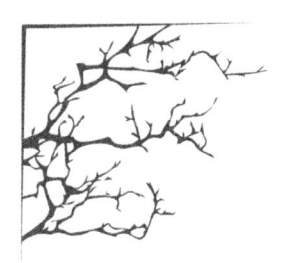

Nod

Just as mirroring is natural for some people on the large scales, so small actions can also convince the subconscious to do your bidding. When most people are actively listening to a conversation, they nod or give signs of verbal agreements. Studies have shown that when you respond with nods when a target speaks, they are more likely to mimic you and nod when asked a favor.

Chapter 8: Responsibility and Ethics

People commonly believe that manipulation is the essence of negative energy, effectively using other people to get gain, but it does not have to be like that. In fact, many people use manipulation for good. Whether it is helping people to get out of a dangerous situation or realizing their self-importance, manipulation can help others overcome adversity and make themselves believe they are worthwhile.

Manipulation can also go too far, however, so it is important to recognize what methods you are using to manipulate someone. If you find yourself making someone feel miserable, analyze the situation and adjust your techniques. All the manipulation tips and tricks listed in this book can be used for good and bad. It is your job to become aware of how your target feels and persuade them gently.

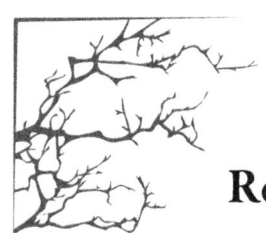

Responsibility

The theory of compatibilism states that humans are not responsible for the actions of another if they do not consciously pull the strings. In other words, if you convince a friend that going on a camping trip would make you feel less connected to them, you are not responsible if they decide to go camping or not. After all, you did not make the decision for them, only provided a possible consequence for their actions.

Someone who wants to complete an action does so of their own accord. The true responsibility in compatibilism comes from the person who has the desire. If someone is compelled to steal because they feel they have no choice, compatibilism may suggest they are not in their right minds, so they are not responsible for their actions.

Television shows endorse the theory of insanity pleas, hoping to get dangerous characters a break from harsher punishments. The lawyers fighting for these criminals use compatibilism as a means to promote the illusion of self-control. If they can convince a jury their client is not right in the mind, they can be absolved from blame.

Manipulators tinker with the lives of those around them, perhaps fine-tuning decisions and placing thoughts in their targets' heads. You may consider yourself to follow the Greek god methods when partaking in others' lives. The Trojan war supposedly began because of an argument about beauty. Aphrodite, Athena, and Hera all asked Paris to decide, based on his supposed fair judgement. In an effort to win praise from Paris, all goddesses offered him a bribe: Athena, the knowledge of battle, Hera, the power to take over the world, and Aphrodite, the love of the most beautiful mortal woman.

Of course, this farce was the basis for the Trojan war, which resulted in Paris's abduction of Helen. Though quite an epic, Paris's decisions were ultimately his own and caused him to start one of the bloodiest wars in legend. The casting of blame is common among immature people who do not wish to take responsibility.

However, true manipulation combats this way of thinking. Even though someone wants to want something, they are not necessarily absolved of blame when their choice leads to actions. Think about it this way: if you ask Sam to go to the movies instead of studying all night, he is still responsible for the choice made. If he chooses not to study, he must face the consequences. So, manipulation, though providing a profound influence on others, does not ultimately absolve them of consequences.

True manipulation is the practice of persuasion, not exploitation. You may convince a brother to think he would be better off with a different girlfriend, but it is he who is responsible for ending the relationship. Exploiters change the way people think and use their vulnerabilities against victims. Often, exploiters tear down their victims with such ferocity that they cannot gain the mental faculties to recover.

Moral Gray Areas

However, what if there are moral gray areas affecting your judgement? Take, for example, the story of Judy who is aiding a friend stuck in a bad relationship. Her friend, Liza, has lived with her boyfriend for five years. He has both mentally and physically abused Liza for three of those years, making Liza believe it is her fault for his change. She feels stuck in a relationship where she is dependent on her boyfriend for both financial and emotional needs.

Judy sees the mental and physical abuse and tries to convince Liza to leave. However, Liza is fully under the control of her boyfriend and does not wish to leave. In a fit of anger, Judy decides to use manipulation to affect the relationship between Liza and her boyfriend.

First, Judy uses reverse psychology to convince the boyfriend that he wants to leave the relationship for something better. She tells the boyfriend that he has not already sucked Liza dry from his constant abuse, and that she can be under his control for longer and receive better results if he stays. Judy then uses subliminal messaging to convince Liza that she is in a bad relationship by associating the word "bad" with name calling.

Though the results could go either way, the boyfriend eventually decides to leave, and Liza is convinced that an abusive relationship is a bad relationship. Judy's use of manipulation ultimately got her friend out of a bad situation, but at what cost?

In all reality, the boyfriend probably used even more abusive language and actions to get Liza to do what he wanted. He probably further cemented Liza's belief that she was only good for someone who was abusive. Judy did release her friend from an abusive boyfriend, but Liza likely moved on to another. Since Judy used dark triad tactics to manipulate both parties, her efforts were successful, but she, ultimately, was not.

So, do the ends of manipulation justify the means? Philosophy is generally mixed on this issue. Judy may have saved Liza's life, but she may also have severely confused Liza by instigating mixed messages. Judy's methods likely needed reevaluation before she went through with her plans.

Morally gray areas are common in reality. In fact, more manipulation is morally gray than black and white. You will seldom manipulate someone with completely beneficial results. After all, you are changing the way someone thinks. Though you may not be responsible for their actions, you are responsible for the way they think.

Those who maintain that morality should be free of manipulation believe that any interference on the part of Judy should have come from a different direction. Morality monitors believe that, because Liza's autonomy was compromised, she was treated unethically. Any interference on Judy's end forcing Liza to think differently was a breach of ethics.

Now, let us look at an example with Alex and his wife Susan. They had been married for 10 years, each of them completely devoted to one another. However, their passion began to wane slightly, and friends and family could see they were struggling. They now slept in different rooms, and Susan did not get up to wish her husband goodbye when he went to work in the morning. Often, Susan would be asleep or locked in her room when Alex returned home.

Friends and family began to intervene by using covert manipulation. They used semantic priming, relating the word "marriage" to happiness. They also tried to appeal to their senses of love for one another by encouraging both Alex and Susan to give gifts to one another. Another friend suggested they use the Benjamin Franklin effect to coerce the two into reminding themselves they were in love with each other.

None of these actions had a negative effect on the two of them. In fact, they did decide to give the marriage another chance, instead spending more time together and taking vacations to renew their spark. They were not left with negative feelings toward one another, and the results of the manipulation did not encourage either of them to feel abused. However, is this method of manipulation ethical?

Many people would say yes. After all, you are not hurting them physically or mentally, so what is the harm? It may have done more good than bad. However, is it ever ethical to change others' minds? The two might have been better off away from each other for days, weeks, months, or years, eventually deciding to stick together or split. The nature of their relationship may have run its course and the meddling of others may have helped in the short term, but Alex and Susan may have ultimately decided that the marriage was not worth the effort.

This is another instance of a morally gray dilemma. How much can you interfere with someone's life before you do more harm than good? If you believe that the two were better off after the interference of family and friends, you will find manipulation easier than those who do not.

The "Thing" Illusion

To justify manipulating others, many start to envision people as things to operate instead of people with whom to interact. This often occurs due to extended use of manipulation. Exploiters use this tactic to distract themselves from seeing a human with autonomy. Narcissists, Machiavellians, and psychopaths use people like their playthings, acting as though the human condition is only the result of pulling theoretical levers. Without constraint, it is easy to fall into this trap.

Even if you have good intentions, seeing people as merely objects to manipulate is philosophically wrong. Human elements are taken out of the equation, which often means the human element of the manipulator. Manipulation becomes a series of moves and countermoves, similar to a chess match.

Manipulators who have followed this path have stopped thinking about how to change someone's opinions by interaction. Therapists who have spent too much time solving the same problems can enter this mechanical mode, manipulating people to do what they deem is right based on what has worked in the past. This response is a sign of a highly intelligent person, but they seriously lack the ability to emotionally connect with others.

Further Considerations

There is no definitive right or wrong when considering how to manipulate someone into doing what you want. You and your target may find it fun to see how much you can influence each other without the other noticing or you may be involved in a relationship that is highly toxic and exists for the benefit of one person only. Whatever the reason, there is an ethical dilemma regarding how to improve lives without sacrificing your target's autonomy.

People vs. Situations

This book has already discussed how to manipulate people by affecting their belief, but, there is another form of manipulation, called environmental manipulation. Manipulation of an environment effectively plays the system without changing the beliefs of another person.

For example, if Rita wants to enter a mental institution but her psychiatrist believes that institution would do more damage than good, Rita may change the rules of the game to force the psychiatrist to admit her. One day, she decides to feign a suicide attempt by standing on the ledge of a building. Her psychiatrist knows that Rita is pulling a stunt and will not really jump, but a police officer has to perform his duty by forcing the psychiatrist to send Rita away.

In this scenario, Rita did not affect the sensibilities of the psychiatrist. Instead, she challenged the beliefs of the police officer, which forced the psychiatrist to react according to the law, effectively using environmental manipulation to meet her goal. She did not manipulate others, so her manipulation practices are morally gray.

Some consider situational or environmental manipulation is ethical because it simply limits choices. When someone threatens to withdraw friendship due to a perceived slight, the manipulation does not immediately change the beliefs of the victim, only the choices. In most cases, many people would find this method ethically reprehensible, but the justification the victim makes is entirely their own.

Vulnerability Manipulation

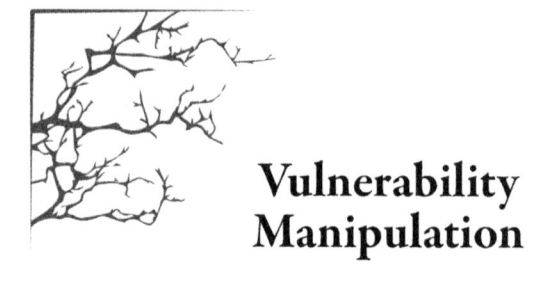

Forcing someone to change beliefs as a form of power play is nothing new. Monarchies and dictatorships have been using these tactics for millennia. However, a new form of vulnerability manipulation has surfaced over the years in the form of gaslighting. Gaslighting is the means of manipulation to make victims feel as though they are going insane. The movie *Gaslight* in 1944 used this principle; the main character terrorized his wife until she did not know what was real.

Gaslighters are notorious liars, and they use large lies to confuse. Some of the lies they tell their victims are so outrageous that they are easily detected, but they continue to follow a pattern of lying that makes their victims question whether or not they are receiving the truth. When victims catch them in the lies, they deny everything, often accusing their victims of sabotage or defamation of character. Victims then become confused, unsure if what they know to be true is reality.

Gaslighters wear their victims down over time. The more lies they tell, the more people they take down in an attempt to make you question your sanity. Victims are caught in the manipulation slowly, like a frog in a frying pan, slowly cooking, though they do not recognize it immediately. Even the most intelligent people can get sucked in.

SUGGESTION: SECRETS OF COVERT MANIPULATION

Manipulators that use vulnerability tactics include psychological and emotional warfare, stopping their tactics to give their victims positive reinforcement. They make their victims confused, which also translates to weakness. The roller coaster of emotions that their victims feel is primary to a gaslighter's plan. Gaslighters aim to maintain emotional instability, making you feel as though instability is normal.

Gaslighters are often so good at what they do that they can convince anyone to turn against their victims. They choose highly loyal people who will back them in whatever they say or do. However, gaslighters do not need these people, only their existence, since they lie to their victims, making their targets believe everyone is against them. Isolation is key to gaslighters, since they need the security of knowing that their victims have nowhere to run.

Even beginner manipulators can fall into these traps by becoming too involved in the end product and not in their targets. The idealization of power that comes from making someone do whatever they want is enough to make most manipulators go a step too far with their victims.

People who are especially vulnerable are told to try drastic measures to make a stand in the world. Women are often told they must fight against more powerful people to be considered human, though this statement is, in itself, another form of manipulation. To become aware of power-hungry tactics, you must be aware of and married to the ideals of pure intent.

5 Golden Questions of Intent

Everyone can get caught up in feeling powerful or enjoying the power that comes from understanding manipulation. However, to remain ethical in manipulation, you must be aware of how you influence others. Answer these questions when beginning a manipulation campaign.

1. What is my goal and who does it benefit?

If your answer reflects that the only one who benefits from manipulation is you, rethink your strategies. There are less detrimental ways to approach a change in behavior. First, analyze the personality characteristics of your target, then move to tactics that would work the best.

For someone who is mentally and emotionally strong, using love flooding will not be as effective as using commitment and consistency. The way you behave around your target will cement your relationship with them without compromising their mental well-being. Someone who has trouble with self-esteem, on the other hand, may benefit from love flooding, as they will feel better when someone recognizes their worth.

1. Do I feel good about this?

Your first instinct is usually the best. If you do not feel good about approaching someone with manipulation tactics, do not do it. However, if you feel like you have your target's best interest in mind, it may be worth it to try manipulation.

However, this often becomes a slippery slope. If your gut reaction is to manipulate someone but you come to realize that they had been the victims of abuses in the past, you may be making their life worse. Before you start your plan, do some research about your target. Knowing your target beforehand is beneficial to your manipulation and in helping them in the future.

Enlist the help of those around them. If your target is in an abusive relationship, it is likely that their family and friends have been aware of the situation and have tried to help the victim in the past. They will know how to help you reach your target and find a way for them to listen.

1. *Am I being completely honest?*

Though some manipulators use lying as a means to an end, manipulators looking to help their targets should strive for honesty. One of the first steps in manipulation is to get close to your target, and the only way to do this is through sincerity. Use this to your advantage and prove yourself a true friend.

Also remember to be honest with yourself. It is common to slip into a puppeteer routine, simply pulling the victim's strings instead of helping them. If you are honest about how you are using your manipulation, you may come to realize that your manipulation strategies are harmful to your target. Good intentions that lead to actions like guilt inducement make matters worse. If you are honest about how you are making your target feel, you can quickly change tactics.

1. *Will this ultimately benefit my target?*

It is easy to get caught up in the idea that what you are doing is good for yourself and other people. However, if you find yourself serving your own purposes instead of those of your target, stop. You want your target to feel joy at the end of your manipulation instead of feeling as though they wasted time on you.

Imagine, for example, that Henry and Tina wanted to get married but had only been dating for a few months. In order to help them, you decide to manipulate them separately to find out if they are truly right for each other. However, as you are working, you notice that you start to develop feelings for Tina. Instead of benefiting the couple, you decide to go after Tina.

In this situation, you started off with the best of intentions, but you forgot those along the way. It is wise to frequently take stock of how you are helping or hurting those you manipulate. After all, intentions change.

1. *Will this develop trust?*

For someone who struggles to find their self-worth, it can be tempting to use manipulation tactics to make them feel better about themselves. However, those good intentions can lead to bad consequences if you are not careful. Your compliments may be construed as ways to manipulate your target. They may

SUGGESTION: SECRETS OF COVERT MANIPULATION

fear you have been love flooding them to give them some fake sense of self-worth that was not warranted.

Instead, take the time to truly get to know your target. When you become closer, you develop true feelings of friendship and trust. Do not go behind your target's back, even if you believe it is for their own good. You are not responsible for their feelings, so just make them feel wanted when they want to open up. If they believe you are not helping for your own ends, you can build a healthy relationship.

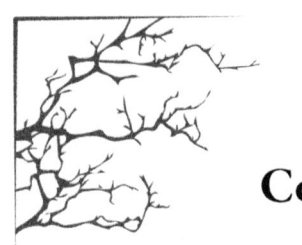

Conclusion

People have been manipulating others for millennia. One of the most shocking examples occurred at the beginning of the 12th century and lasted for several hundred years, known as the Inquisition. Perhaps the most terrible accounts, however, happened in Spain and started a tradition of brutality to get information.

The Inquisition was responsible for sniffing out heresies. Anyone who blasphemed or held a belief contrary to the Catholic Church was punished for their crimes. In most cases, this involved anything from a whipping to exile, but those who found their places in the Inquisition often delighted in the torture of others and manipulated confessions through extreme torture.

Under the rule of Torquemada, many people were forced to confess to heresy, despite little evidence. If they confessed, they were tortured for their crimes. If they did not, they were burned at the stake. When Diego de Deza rose to power as the Grand Inquisitor, people would suffer much worse fates, such as imprisonment and death.

Inquisitors were able to manipulate people into confessing to crimes they did not commit, just to avoid a worse fate. Though some people use methods to manipulate others today, science has made the endeavor far more humane and realistic.

SUGGESTION: SECRETS OF COVERT MANIPULATION

People are not forced into confessions through brute force. Today's manipulation lies in the mind.

Manipulation is the art of changing the minds and beliefs of another for your or their gain. Whether you want to influence your friends to help them or change the way that others think about your products, there is always some that catches the eyes of others, tricking their minds into believing you want what a manipulator wants.

Narcissism, psychopathy, and Machiavellianism are the three corners of the dark triad from which dark psychology arises. Narcissists are focused mostly on themselves and do not often see the benefit of interacting with others, psychopaths are devoid of empathy and use charm as a cover for their brutal natures, and Machiavellians seek only for their success. All three use mind control techniques to achieve what they want. The techniques they use can also be used to trick others' brains. The simple art of suggestion is often enough to make someone believe manipulators are reading their minds.

Before you can start to manipulate others, you must first know yourself. This includes deep introspection to determine what your true desires are. The only way to achieve this is through honesty. When you are honest with yourself about your true motives, you open a window to your soul that helps you understand why you behave the way you do. Identify your insecurities, fears, problems, and vulnerabilities. Accept what you find without judgement. Self-judgement leads to self-denial, closing your mind. Find out how the world affects you. You can find out how events in your life affect you by meditating daily.

When you have discovered who you are, learn how to modify your behavior. In order to manipulate others, you need to be able to understand how to assimilate yourself into their lives. Taking acting and debate classes will help you understand how to effectively mirror someone without detection. Working on your charms can bring targets to you. However, the best way to modify your behavior is to follow master manipulators and copy their actions.

The next step is to understand others. The five big personality traits—agreeableness, openness, conscientiousness, extraversion, and neuroticism—help you identify what tactics work best. Understanding the extremes of these personality traits make it easier for you to gain trust. After you have entered your target's inner circle, find out their true desires. They will eagerly tell you if you make it known that you are sincere. Develop a similarity with your target to ensure they will like you.

Use emotions to change how others behave. The basic emotions of fear, anger, sadness, and happiness trigger bodily reactions, often affecting the brain. If you capitalize on others' emotions, you can more effectively change their beliefs. Use love flooding by showering your target with love and gifts. When you pair love flooding with denial, your target becomes trapped in a never-ending loop. Passive-aggressive behavior, which often includes guilt inducement, forces your target to second guess themselves. They will develop a dependency on your crazy switches of behavior, falling further under your spell.

Use words to change the way a person thinks. Words are extremely powerful, and convincing someone of their dependence on you can keep them coming back to you time and

SUGGESTION: SECRETS OF COVERT MANIPULATION

again. Use confusion techniques to speak with their subconscious minds. Put ideas into your target's head, making them believe they are acting on their own thoughts. Restrict choices by limiting options and using leading questions. Sarcasm and lying break down a person's will due to their subtle cruelties.

Reverse psychology makes others believe you want the opposite of your actual intentions. By denying your desire, you can convince targets to do your bidding. Confrontational people are the best subjects as they are usually volatile. By using logic, you can convince a neurotic person that they want the opposite of their true wishes.

Subliminal influence is most common in marketing, but you can also use it to condition others to behave how you expect. The art of priming is a long-haul approach. Through semantic, visual, and positive and negative priming, you can condition your target to believe what you are doing is for their best interest. Also consider the Benjamin Franklin effect by getting someone to do a favor for you. When asking for a favor, ask for a large one first, then scale it back later. As always, induce your target's response by nodding to make them nod.

Manipulation takes a great deal of responsibility. You are affecting the way another person behaves and thinks, changing their autonomy. Therefore, avoid abusing your power. Gaslighting is the culmination of power tactics, making your target believe they are going insane. Always be responsible when manipulating others.

Find out who you truly are and do your best for humankind. Remember, manipulation can be used for good, and it should be used that way. If you follow the principles in this book, you can convince anyone of anything.

Thank you so much for reading this book and do not forget to give it a favorable review when you stop back at Amazon.

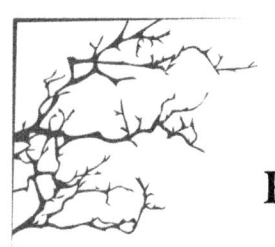

References

Bilotta, E., Carcione, A., Fera, T., Moroni, F., Nicolò, G., Pedone, R., ... Colle, L. (2018). Symptom severity and mindreading in narcissistic personality disorder. *PLOS ONE*, 13(8). https://doi.org/10.1371/journal.pone.0201216

Biography.com. (2019, September 4). Joseph Stalin. https://www.biography.com/dictator/joseph-stalin

Bradberry, T. (n.d.). 13 habits of exceptionally likeable people. https://www.talentsmart.com/articles/13-Habits-of-Exceptionally-Likeable-People-507024439-p-1.html

brain+. (2019, November 1). Illusions & brain benders: How your mind plays tricks on you. https://www.brain-plus.com/illusions__brain-benders-mind-plays-tricks/

Brewer, G., & Abell, L. (2017). Machiavellianism, relationship satisfaction, and romantic relationship quality. *Europe's Journal of Psychology*, 13(3), 491–502. https://doi.org/10.5964/ejop.v13i3.1217

Brogaard, B. (2016, November 13). 5 signs you're dealing with a passive aggressive person. https://www.psychologytoday.com/us/blog/the-superhuman-mind/201611/5-signs-youre-dealing-passive-aggressive-person

Brown, L. (2018, December 11). The truth of reverse psychology and 4 steps to mastering it. https://hackspirit.com/reverse-psychology/

Buczynski, R., PhD. (2020, March 23). How anger affects the brain and body [Infographic]. https://www.nicabm.com/how-anger-affects-the-brain-and-body-infographic/

Chakravorty, S. (2018, May 3). How to be a good debater. https://www.careerindia.com/tips/how-to-be-a-good-debater-022568.html

Cherry, K. (2020a, January 23). How absolute threshold of a stimulus is used in experimental research. https://www.verywellmind.com/what-is-the-absolute-threshold-2795221

Cherry, K. (2020b, February 21). Priming and the psychology of memory. https://www.verywellmind.com/priming-and-the-psychology-of-memory-4173092

Cherry, K. (2020c, March 8). How to Recognize the Signs That Someone Is Lying. https://www.verywellmind.com/how-to-tell-if-someone-is-lying-2795917

Cialdini, R. (2019, June 25). The 6 principles of persuasion. https://www.influenceatwork.com/principles-of-persuasion/

Colaianni, P. (2019, October 10). Confusing you into submission: A common manipulation you may fall for again and again. https://loveandabuse.com/confusing-you-into-submission-a-common-manipulation-you-may-fall-for-again-and-again/

Cyr, I. (2019, February 5). Manipulation and moral responsibility. https://1000wordphilosophy.com/2019/02/05/manipulation-and-moral-responsibility/

Dachis, A. (2014, October 21). How to plant ideas in someone's mind. https://lifehacker.com/how-to-plant-ideas-in-someones-mind-5715912

Davies, B. J. A. (2018, November 23). A master manipulator will do these 6 things – Are you dealing with one? https://www.learning-mind.com/master-manipulator/

Davis, S. (2019, April 11). The neuroscience of shame. https://cptsdfoundation.org/2019/04/11/the-neuroscience-of-shame/

Degges-White, S. (2018, April 13). Love bombing: A narcissist's secret weapon. https://www.psychologytoday.com/us/blog/lifetime-connections/201804/love-bombing-narcissists-secret-weapon

Dhyanse. (2019, January 2). Who am I: A self discovery guided meditation to reveal your inner truth. https://www.dhyanse.com/2019/01/02/who-am-i-a-self-discovery-guided-meditation-to-reveal-your-inner-truth/

Effectiviology. (n.d.). The Benjamin Franklin effect: How to build rapport by asking for favors. https://effectiviology.com/benjamin-franklin-effect/

Elgendi, M., Kumar, P., Barbic, S., Howard, N., Abbott, D., & Cichocki, A. (2018). Subliminal priming—State of the art and future perspectives. *Behavioral Sciences*, 8(6), 54. https://doi.org/10.3390/bs8060054

Fonseca, T. A. (n.d.). Mirroring body language: 4 steps to successfully mirror others. https://scienceofpeople.com/mirroring/

Gauthier, I. (2000). Visual priming: The ups and downs of familiarity. *Current Biology*, 10(20), R753–R756. https://doi.org/10.1016/s0960-9822(00)00738-7

Gertler, B. (2015, May 18). Self-Knowledge (Stanford Encyclopedia of Philosophy). https://plato.stanford.edu/entries/self-knowledge/

Glicksman, E. (2019, September 12). Your brain on guilt and shame. https://www.brainfacts.org/thinking-sensing-and-behaving/emotions-stress-and-anxiety/2019/your-brain-on-guilt-and-shame-091219

Greenberg, M. (2012, March 14). 10 ways your supermarket hijacks your brain. https://www.psychologytoday.com/us/blog/the-mindful-self-express/201203/10-ways-your-supermarket-hijacks-your-brain

Hartley, D. (2015, September 8). Meet the Machiavellians. https://www.psychologytoday.com/us/blog/machiavellians-gulling-the-rubes/201509/meet-the-machiavellians

Help Guide. (2020, March 13). Benefits of mindfulness. https://www.helpguide.org/harvard/benefits-of-mindfulness.htm

History.com. (2018, August 21). Inquisition. https://www.history.com/topics/religion/inquisition

History.com. (2019a, June 10). Ethnic cleansing. https://www.history.com/topics/holocaust/ethnic-cleansing

History.com. (2019b, October 8). Salem Witch Trials. https://www.history.com/topics/colonial-america/salem-witch-trials

Jacobson, S. (2015, January 8). What is Machiavellianism in psychology? https://www.harleytherapy.co.uk/counselling/machiavellianism-psychology.htm

Jalili, C. (2019, August 21). How to tell if someone is lying to you, according to body language experts. https://time.com/5443204/signs-lying-body-language-experts/

Javanbahkt, A., & Saab, L. (2017, October 27). What happens in the brain when we feel fear. https://www.smithsonianmag.com/science-nature/what-happens-brain-feel-fear-180966992/

Jones, J. (2018, December 21). How to master the skill of persuasion. http://drjasonjones.com/master_skill_persuasion/

Jones, J. (2019a, September 7). Dark psychology & manipulation: Are you unknowingly using them? http://drjasonjones.com/dark_psychology/

Jones, J. (2019b, September 7). How to avoid being manipulated. http://drjasonjones.com/how-to-avoid-being-manipulated/

Kacel, E. L., Ennis, N., & Pereira, D. B. (2017). Narcissistic personality disorder in clinical health psychology practice: Case studies of comorbid psychological distress and life-limiting illness. *Behavioral Medicine*, 43(3), 156–164. https://doi.org/10.1080/08964289.2017.1301875

Kanev, T. (2017, April 24). Perception and how it is used for marketing. http://thenovicemarketeer.com/perception-and-how-it-is-used-in-marketing/

Kauppinen, A. (2014, January 29). Moral sentimentalism. https://plato.stanford.edu/entries/moral-sentimentalism/

Kiehl, K. A., & Hoffman, M. B. (2014). The criminal psychopath: History, neuroscience, treatment, and economics. Jurimetrics, (51), 355–397. https://www.ncbi.nlm.nih.gov/pmc/articles/PMC4059069/

Lancer, D. (2018, December 10). Beware of the malevolent dark triad. https://www.psychologytoday.com/us/blog/toxic-relationships/201812/beware-the-malevolent-dark-triad

Lazarus, C. N. (2012, June 26). Think sarcasm is funny? Think again. https://www.psychologytoday.com/us/blog/think-well/201206/think-sarcasm-is-funny-think-again

Learn subliminal messages you can use to influence people. (2013, June 3). https://leadingpersonality.wordpress.com/2013/06/03/learn-subliminal-messages-you-can-use-to-influence-people/

Markarian, T. (2018, January 17). How the most infamous dictators in history fooled their people. https://www.grunge.com/60925/infamous-dictators-history-fooled-people/

McKay, K. B. &. (2019, July 16). The 3 elements of charisma: Presence. https://www.artofmanliness.com/articles/the-3-elements-of-charisma-presence/

Melchers, M. C., Li, M., Haas, B. W., Reuter, M., Bischoff, L., & Montag, C. (2016). Similar personality patterns are associated with empathy in four different countries. *Frontiers in Psychology*, 7. https://doi.org/10.3389/fpsyg.2016.00290

Nicholson, J. (2012, February 8). How to influence and persuade with touch. https://www.psychologytoday.com/us/blog/the-attraction-doctor/201202/how-influence-and-persuade-touch

Nuccetelli, A. (2019, October 12). Dark psychology - Dark side of human consciousness concept. https://www.ipredator.co/dark-psychology/

Pantalon, M. (2011, April 8). Do you use "reverse psychology"? Stop right now! https://www.psychologytoday.com/intl/blog/the-science-influence/201104/do-you-use-reverse-psychology-stop-right-now

Perry, P. (2019, March 16). Why is it you can sense when someone's staring at you? https://bigthink.com/philip-perry/why-is-it-you-can-sense-when-someones-staring-at-you

Psychology Behind. (2019, August 26). Psychology behind the art of manipulation. https://medium.com/@PsychBehind/psychology-behind-the-art-of-manipulation-d9e0bdd6d8d3

Quora. (n.d.). Who was the most manipulative person in our history? https://www.quora.com/Who-was-the-most-manipulative-person-in-our-history

Quora. (2017, March 19). How to use psychology to manipulate people. https://www.quora.com/How-can-you-use-psychology-to-manipulate-people

Sarkis, S. A. (2017, January 22). 11 warning signs of gaslighting. https://www.psychologytoday.com/us/blog/here-there-and-everywhere/201701/11-warning-signs-gaslighting

Schneider, A. (2018, February 7). Silent treatment: Preferred weapon of people with narcissism. https://www.goodtherapy.org/blog/silent-treatment-a-narcissistic-persons-preferred-weapon-0602145

Schwitzgebel, E. (2019, October 18). Introspection. https://plato.stanford.edu/archives/win2019/entries/introspection/

Smith, K. (2018, August 7). 7 ways to spot a lie. https://psychcentral.com/blog/7-ways-to-spot-a-lie/

Stanford Encyclopedia of Philosophy. (2018, March 30). The ethics of manipulation. https://plato.stanford.edu/entries/ethics-manipulation/

Stern, V. (2015, September 1). A short history of the rise, fall and rise of subliminal messaging. https://www.scientificamerican.com/article/a-short-history-of-the-rise-fall-and-rise-of-subliminal-messaging/?error=cookies_not_supported&code=92b803d6-6f21-4b68-bdfe-982f1e65845d

TED. (2008, July 21). Brain magic | Keith Barry [Video file]. https://www.youtube.com/watch?v=GigYWy2UmOY

TEDx Talks. (2016, May 3). Fear, anger and how to counter the manipulation of the human mind

| Nicole LeFavour | TEDxBoise [Video file]. https://www.youtube.com/watch?v=xa1RShs7wyI

Tipper, S. P. (2008, February 13). Negative priming. http://www.scholarpedia.org/article/Negative_priming

Tyrrell, M. (2019, August 15). The hypnotic art of confusion. https://www.unk.com/blog/the-hypnotic-art-of-confusion/

van Edwards, V. (n.d.). What is curiosity? The science of curiosity in our brains. https://www.scienceofpeople.com/curiosity/

Wang, L. Z. (2018, March 17). Are you being manipulated by subliminal messages? [infographic]. https://medium.com/behavior-design/are-you-being-manipulated-by-subliminal-messages-infographic-39ce82143c56

Waude, A. (2017a, February 2). Extraversion and introversion. https://www.psychologistworld.com/influence-personality/extraversion-introversion

Waude, A. (2017b, March 7). Openness to experience: A "big five" personality trait. https://www.psychologistworld.com/influence-personality/openness-to-experience-trait

Waude, A. (2017c, April 12). Conscientiousness, personality and behavior. https://www.psychologistworld.com/influence-personality/conscientiousness-personality-trait

Waude, A. (2017d, April 27). Agreeableness: A "big five" personality factor. https://www.psychologistworld.com/personality/agreeableness-personality-trait

Waude, A. (2017e, May 4). Neuroticism: A "big five" personality factor. https://www.psychologistworld.com/personality/neuroticism-personality-trait

Weber, J. P. (2015, January 29). 5 ways to get closer. https://www.psychologytoday.com/us/blog/having-sex-wanting-intimacy/201501/5-ways-get-closer

wikiHow. (2020a, February 1). How to use reverse psychology. https://www.wikihow.com/Use-Reverse-Psychology

wikiHow. (2020b, February 5). How to manipulate people. https://www.wikihow.com/Manipulate-People

Wolff, C. (2017, May 31). 11 ways to get your partner to open up, if you think they rarely share their true feelings. https://www.bustle.com/p/11-ways-to-get-your-partner-to-open-up-if-you-think-they-rarely-share-their-true-feelings-61197

Wood, K. (2013, August 19). The lost art of introspection: Why you must master yourself . https://expertenough.com/2990/the-lost-art-of-introspection-why-you-must-master-yourself

Zwilling, M. (2011, May 25). Seven ways to make people feel important. https://www.huffpost.com/entry/seven-ways-to-make-people_b_684768

Did you love *Suggestion: Secrets of Covert Manipulation*? Then you should read *How To Analyze People at a Glance - Learn 15 Unmistakable Signals Others Put Off Without Realizing It and What They Mean*[1] by Leo Black!

Would You Want to Know What Others Are Thinking about You with 100% Certainty?

It's inevitable to feel like someone is attempting to tell you no, even when their words point towards "yes."

As humans, **we don't always say what we mean** and we don't always mean what we say.

Communication is complex, intricate and full of layers.

---

1. https://books2read.com/u/4AzWAN

2. https://books2read.com/u/4AzWAN

Just take a look at the following incredible facts:

55% of communication hides in body language and **non-verbal cues**Sight accounts for approximately 82% of how we take in informationResearchers have identified **19 different types of human smiles**, each one with its meaning!The amount of non-verbal communication that we engage in on a daily basis varies between 60 and 90 percentTo keep an audience engaged when speaking, you have to maintain eye contact for at least 60% of the time

That's a lot to take in, isn't it?

Adding cultural specific and personal nuances makes the situation even more complicated.

So the question remains – **is it possible to read people accurately and respond adequately to their signals?**

The answer is an obvious yes. You will, however, need to engage in some self-analysis and you'll also have to pay attention to others. Once you become more present in everyday interactions, you will begin pinpointing cues and patterns of behavior that reveal a ton more than spoken word will ever be capable of.

To read people, you have to be **attentive and emotionally intelligent.** Both of these can be learned, boosting your confidence and helping you form more meaningful relationships.

In *How to Analyze People at a Glance,* you will discover:

The number one reason why **non-verbal communication** is so much **more important** than spoken words7 **codes** of non-verbal communication everybody should masterA surefire way to determine if others are being deceitfulThe meaning of body language – when words say one thing and the body's telling you something elsePractical strategies for **differentiating** between **positive** and **negative** body languageSome of the most common signals people give and their meaningPutting the theory of analyzing people to use in your personal relationships**Powerful techniques for influencing others and making them like you**The basics of neuro-linguistic programmingThe fine difference between being **persuasive** and being **manipulative**

And a lot more.

As humans, we are all flawed, we're all insecure and we're all looking for a deeper connection. Sometimes, however, we go about it in the worst possible way.

How to Analyze People will teach you how to go beyond shallow communication and how to look deep into the actions and motivations of others. Equipped with this knowledge, you will excel in your career, you will make new friends and achieve a level of life satisfaction you've probably considered impossible in the past.

Every human being is an open book if you understand its language. If you want to start reading others and responding to their cues better, scroll up and click the "Add to Cart" button now.

Also by Leo Black

How To Analyze People at a Glance - Learn 15 Unmistakable Signals Others Put Off Without Realizing It and What They Mean

Suggestion: Secrets of Covert Manipulation

Printed in Great Britain
by Amazon